Hope Restored

The Walter Brueggemann Library

Davis Hankins, *Editor*

Other books in this series:

Deliver Us: Salvation and the Liberating God of the Bible

Our Hearts Wait: Worshiping through Praise and Lament in the Psalms

Hope Restored

Biblical Imagination against Empire

Walter Brueggemann

WESTMINSTER
JOHN KNOX PRESS
LOUISVILLE · KENTUCKY

First edition
Published by Westminster John Knox Press
Louisville, Kentucky

23 24 25 26 27 28 29 30 31 32—10 9 8 7 6 5 4 3 2 1

Book design by Sharon Adams
Cover design by designpointinc.com

Library of Congress Cataloging-in-Publication Data is on file
at the Library of Congress, Washington, DC.

ISBN-13: 978-0-664-26590-8

*We happily dedicate this volume to our
teachers, advisors, mentors, and advocates,
James Muilenburg (Brueggemann) and
Carol Newsom (Hankins). When our hopes flag,
we remember that they hoped in us.*

Contents

Series Preface

I have been very pleased that David Dobson and his staff at Westminster John Knox Press have proposed this extended series of republications of my work. Indeed, I know of no old person who is not pleased to be taken seriously in old age! My first thought, in learning of this proposed series, is that my life and my work have been providentially fortunate in having good companions all along the way who have both supported me and for the most part kept me honest in my work. I have been blessed by the best teachers, who have prepared me to think both critically and generatively. I have been fortunate to be accompanied by good colleagues, both academic and pastoral, who have engaged my work. And I have been gifted to have uncommonly able students, some of whom continue to instruct me in the high art of Old Testament study.

The long years of my work that will be represented in this series reflect my slow process of finding my own voice, of sorting out accents and emphases, and of centering my work on recurring themes that I have judged to merit continuing attention. The result of that slow process is that over time my work is marked by repetition and reiteration, as well as contradiction, change of mind, and ambiguity, all of which belong to seeing my work as an organic whole as I have been given courage and insight. In the end I have settled on recurring themes (reflected in the organization of this series) that I hope I have continued to treat with imagination, so that my return to them is not simply reiteration but is critically generative of new perspective and possibility.

In retrospect I can identify two learnings from the philosopher and hermeneut Paul Ricoeur that illumine my work. Ricoeur has given me names for what I have been doing, even though I was at work on such matters before I acquired Ricoeur's terminology. First, in his book *Freud and Philosophy* (1965), Ricoeur identifies two moves that are essential for interpretation. On the one hand there is "suspicion." By this term Ricoeur means critical skepticism. In biblical study "suspicion" has taken the form of historical criticism, in which the interpreter doubts the "fictive" location and function of the text and hypothesizes about the "real, historical" location and function of the text. On the other hand there is "retrieval," by which Ricoeur means the capacity to reclaim what is true in the text after due "suspicion." My own work has included measures of "suspicion," because a grounding in historical criticism has been indispensable for responsible interpretation. My work, however, is very much and increasingly tilted toward "retrieval," the recovery of what is theologically urgent in the text. My own location in a liberal-progressive trajectory of interpretation has led me to an awareness that liberal-progressives are tempted to discard "the baby" along with "the bath." For that reason my work has been to recover and reclaim, I hope in generative imaginative ways, the claims of biblical faith.

Second and closely related, Ricoeur has often worked with a grid of "precritical/critical/postcritical" interpretation. My own schooling and that of my companions has been in a critical tradition; that enterprise by itself, however, has left the church with little to preach, teach, or trust. For that reason my work has become increasingly postcritical, that is, with a "second naiveté," a readiness to engage in serious ways the claims of the text. I have done so in a conviction that the alternative metanarratives available to us are inadequate and the core claims of the Bible are more adequate for a life of responsible well-being. Both liberal-progressive Christians and fundamentalist Christians are tempted and seduced by alternative narratives that are elementally inimical to the claims of the Bible; for that reason the work of a generative exposition of biblical claims seems to me urgent. Thus I anticipate that this series may be a continuing invitation to the ongoing urgent work of exposition that both makes clear the singular claims of the Bible and exposes the inadequacy of competing narratives that, from a biblical perspective, amount to idolatry. It is my hope that such continuing work will not only give preachers something substantive to preach and give teachers something substantive to teach, but will invite the church to embrace the biblical claims that it can "trust and obey."

My work has been consistently in response to the several unfolding crises facing our society and, more particularly, the crises faced by the church. Strong market forces and ideological passions that occupy center stage among us sore tempt the church to skew its tradition, to compromise its gospel claim, and to want to be "like the nations" (see 1 Sam. 8:5, 20), that is, without the embarrassment of gospel disjunction. Consequently I have concluded, over time, that our interpretive work must be more radical in its awareness that the claims of faith increasingly contradict the dominant ideologies of our time. That increasing awareness of contradiction is ill-served by progressive-liberal accommodation to capitalist interests or, conversely, it is ill-served by the packaged reductions of reactionary conservatism. The work we have now to do is more complex and more demanding than either progressive-liberal or reactionary-conservative offers. Thus our work is to continue to probe this normative tradition that is entrusted to us that is elusive in its articulation and that hosts a Holy Agent who runs beyond our explanatory categories in irascible freedom and in bottomless fidelity.

I am grateful to the folk at Westminster John Knox and to a host of colleagues who continue to engage my work. I am profoundly grateful to Davis Hankins, on the one hand, for his willingness to do the arduous work of editing this series. On the other hand, I am grateful to Davis for being my conversation partner over time in ways that have evoked some of my better work and that have fueled my imagination in fresh directions. I dare anticipate that this coming series of republication will, in generative ways beyond my ken, continue to engage a rising generation of interpreters in bold, courageous, and glad obedience.

Walter Brueggemann

Editor's Introduction

I began theological education just as Walter Brueggemann was scheduled to retire at Columbia Theological Seminary. I knew very little about the academic study of religion, probably even less about the state of biblical scholarship at the turn of the twenty-first century, yet somehow I knew enough to take every possible course with Dr. Brueggemann. After retiring, Walter continued to teach a course periodically and work from his study on campus—and he always insisted that it and any pastor's work space be called a "study" rather than an "office"! But before he retired, during his last and my first year at Columbia, I took six different courses in biblical studies, including three with Walter. In my memory, I spent that academic year much like St. Thecla as she sat in a windowsill and listened to the teachings of the apostle Paul. According to her mother's descriptive flourish, Thecla, "clinging to the window like a spider, lays hold of what is said by him with a strange eagerness and fearful emotion." It was for me as it had been for Thecla. I imagine my mother would empathize with hers.

Longtime readers as well as those encountering Walter's words for the first time will discover in the volumes of the Walter Brueggemann Library the same soaring rhetoric, engaging intelligence, acute social analysis, moral clarity, wit, generosity, and grace that make it so enlightening and enjoyable to learn from and with Walter Brueggemann. The world we inhabit is broken, dominated by the special interests of the wealthy, teeming with misinformation, divided by entrenched social hierarchies, often despairing before looming ecological catastrophe, and callously indifferent, if not aggressively predatory, toward those facing increasing deprivation and immiseration. In these volumes readers will find Walter at his best, sharply naming these dynamics of brokenness and richly engaging biblical traditions to uncover and chart alternative forms of collective life that promise to be more just, more merciful, and more loving.

Each volume in the Walter Brueggemann Library coheres around a distinct theme that is a prominent concern across Walter's many publications. The contents of the volumes consist of materials taken from a variety of his previously published works. In other words, I have compiled whole chapters or articles, sections, snippets for some volumes, and at times even just a line or two from Walter's publications, and sought to weave them together to create a new book that coheres around a specific theme, in this case the theme of hope in the Bible.

Familiar readers will know that Brueggemann's work is filled with edgy social critique, sharp indictments against rampant corruption, complicity, and indifference. His polemics are aimed especially at the reigning ideas, practices, and values in the global North and West, the United States in particular. But Brueggemann's pointed critiques are never isolated denunciations; they are always laying the groundwork for proposing alternatives. He repeatedly strives to imagine other ways of living, putting forward alternative visions, policy platforms, and defining values for those who are open to and hoping for such alternatives. His *reactions to reject* prevailing ideologies in the West invariably become the baseline for *proactively projecting* the shape, practices, and values characteristic of an alternative social order. For Brueggemann, God is the source and agent who makes such an alternative possible, and in the Bible he discovers revelatory texts that can instruct and inspire communities to hope for and follow that divine agent who is not determined by present arrangements.

Brueggemann's vision of biblical hope functions, first, to distance us from the whole ensemble of resources, technologies, labor, ideas, and social, legal, religious, and political relationships that organize our existence in the world and reproduce it into the future. That is, biblical hope calls out as incomplete and contingent all the ways that our lives are organized, produced, and reproduced—and thus leaves them open to change: "Hope keeps the present arrangement open and provisional" (chap. 2, p. 15). Surprisingly, or unsurprisingly, then, hope emerges primarily among those who grieve the prevailing forces that shape our social life, and who most long for that change. Hope is therefore also an exercise in human creativity and freedom. But enlivening that creativity and freedom to transform the prevailing reality, Brueggemann claims, requires the activation of liberated human imaginations.

Brueggemann's repeated demonstration that hope necessarily involves human imagination is one of his great contributions to our understanding of a specifically biblical hope. Imagination in this sense refers to the dual capacities of human beings both *to perceive* the contradictions, exclusions, and limitations that are produced by the worlds in which they live, and also *to project* other, better realities into those same spaces. And yet Brueggemann consistently distinguishes hope from optimism, evolution, progress, and other similar concepts that can emerge immanently out of present arrangements. For him, the latter are fully compatible with and even at the heart of contemporary social arrangements that are always promising a better future—if only we could be more productive, and if only we could purchase improved, newer, and more commodities. Biblical hope is not grounded in the prevailing system that always promises and never delivers satisfaction from higher productivity and more consumption. Biblical hope is not driven by a desire for personal pleasures but is instead oriented toward what the Bible variously imagines as the common good, a flourishing public world that manifests God's *shalom*.

Brueggemann's approach to the biblical texts is similarly dialectical, attentive to how they, like we, are torn between propagating the status quo and projecting hopeful alternatives. The Bible, like its contemporary communities of interpretation, emerged out of and intervened in particular social contexts; it never simply reflects those contexts, nor is it fully determined by them. This is in part because any social context is contradictory, incomplete—not capable of fully determining anything—and also because the biblical texts themselves are open ended, dynamic, and capable of generating fresh meanings through new interpretations in different times and places. They do not have singular or even precise meanings—a hopeful prospect in itself. In Brueggemann's view, texts should be seen as shaped by but also capable of reshaping particular social formations, open to new meanings and futures. And interpretation should, ultimately, consider how it is also rooted in, and capable of uprooting, the contexts of readers themselves. Brueggemann does all this in these chapters, which is why his work characteristically opens the biblical texts to potential collaborations with religious and political practices. His goals are never simply to grasp the past or even to understand the present, but always also seek to produce critical analyses that might participate in and contribute to future movements for social transformation, both religious and political.

Between two introductory chapters and a concluding chapter, this book is organized according to the traditional Jewish ordering of the canon of books in the Hebrew Bible, with its division into three sections: (i) the first five books (or Pentateuch) of the *Torah* (Genesis, Exodus, Leviticus, Numbers, and Deuteronomy), (ii) the historical and literary works of the *Former and Latter Prophets* (Joshua, Judges, Samuel, and Kings; plus Isaiah, Jeremiah, Ezekiel, and the Twelve Minor Prophets), and (iii) the less cohesive set of texts known as the *Writings* (the remaining eleven books of the Hebrew Bible). Following the introductory chapters 1 and 2 laying the foundation for our understanding of biblical hope in part 1, chapter 3 opens part 2 with a broad analysis of the Torah as a collective act of hopeful imagination that sets out to form a multigenerational community shaped by wonder, the discipline of gratitude, and faithful solidarity. Chapter 3 also includes the first "Midrashic Moment," using the traditional Jewish term for interpretation, in which Brueggemann briefly introduces readers to how a relevant text has been brought into dialogue with a past historical context in ways that have manifested biblical hope. Chapter 3's Midrashic Moment refers to Martin Luther King Jr.'s use of Deuteronomy 34 to depict himself as a new Moses, leading his people to but ultimately not accompanying them into a promised land. Chapter 4 focuses on the early ancestral stories in Genesis narrating the tales of Abraham, Sarah, Hagar, and related characters whose lives were transformed by their faith and hope in God's promises for a radically different future. Parts 3 and 4 (chapters 5 through 9) undertake broader discussions of a larger corpus of literature (as with chapter 3), alongside portions that focus on specific texts within that corpus (as with chapter 4). Sometimes the latter offer close readings of particular passages, designated with the header "Exegetical Focus," in contrast to sections featuring sermons that focus on specific texts, labeled "Homiletical Focus."

Part 3 begins in chapter 5 with another treatment of hope across several biblical books (Joshua, Judges, Samuel, and Kings) that in Jewish tradition are called the Former Prophets. Some readers may initially think of these as historical books, but their designation as "prophets" helpfully reminds us that their stories are told from a theological perspective that construes lived reality as profoundly shaped by the expectations and agency of Israel's God. Jewish tradition includes these books alongside the works associated with prophetic characters like Isaiah, Jeremiah, Ezekiel, and the twelve shorter books, which the tradition calls Latter Prophets. After a short discussion of how the Former Prophets give an account of Israel's life in the promised land that culminates in the loss of their native kingdom and land yet also offers glimmers of hope for an alternative future beyond exile, chapter 5 includes another Midrashic Moment that briefly considers the prominent role played by Elijah in subsequent traditions of imaginative hope, Jewish and Christian alike. The chapter then settles into the latter or literary prophets, delving into some of the most inspiring articulations of hope in the Bible. Chapter 6 offers an exegetical focus on the second half of the book of Isaiah, which includes some of the best poetry in the Bible. In soaring poetic rhetoric, Isaiah dares to proclaim that God has good news (see 40:9; i.e., "gospel") for the deported people: God has resolved to perform a mighty miracle to end exile, restore the people to security in their land, and reopen their future so that they might live hopefully and obediently in restored relationship with their compassionate and forgiving God. Chapter 6 then includes a sermon on Isaiah 62:1–5 and Jesus' miraculous transformation of water into wine in John 2.

Part 4 takes up the topic of hope as it is variously illuminated in a number of books collected in the grab bag of texts known in the Jewish canon as the Writings. After discussing several groupings of texts that find hope in changing circumstances, chapters 7 and 8 focus on Daniel, referred to by Brueggemann as "the quintessential book of hope in the Hebrew Bible" (chap. 7, p. 102) because of the courage and freedom that the protagonists display through their unqualified faith in God's providential care over world events. Chapter 7 takes up the familiar stories in Daniel 2–4, including the antipatriotic yet hopeful story of the fiery furnace in Daniel 3 and the courageously hope-filled interpretations of Nebuchadnezzar's secret and enigmatic dreams, respectively, in Daniel 2 and 4. Chapter 8 then considers the narrative about the Jews' strategically resistant initiation into high Babylonian society in Daniel 1—taking an open and hopeful stance as they learn Babylonian culture, names, and knowledge while remaining unsullied by the empire's junk food—along with the apocalyptic visions in Daniel 7–12, which offer visions of God as a mysterious yet controlling agent over history in whom the faithful may trust and hope. Chapter 9 offers an exegetical and homiletical focus on the psalms of lament, which occupy nearly one-third of the Psalms. If Daniel is the quintessential book of hope, the lament psalms are the paradigmatic poems of hope, moving the reader from dire need, danger, and despair, to hope, joy, and thanksgiving. The sermon at the end of the chapter brings this movement to life through the surprising parable Jesus tells in Luke 18:1–8 about a destitute woman who pesters an indifferent judge until he grants her the justice that she had been denied; her insistent appeals, Brueggemann suggests, are a belated version of the prayers that one finds in the lament psalms.

Finally, the book concludes with a chapter that is ostensibly on "missionary preaching," yet is directly tied to our theme of hope. Brueggemann defines missionary preaching as the articulation of and invitation to participate in the radically alternative kingdom of God, and ranges across much of the Old Testament to show how different texts and traditions articulate biblical hope in a variety of distinct themes, concepts, and metaphors that prevent the stifling of interpretive imagination.

On the heels (we hope) of a global pandemic, amidst havoc wrought by increasingly extreme climate change, in the context of ongoing war, violence against Black and brown bodies by state agents and rogue terrorists, a surge in anti-Semitism and fascism around the world, the ever-widening chasm between superrich billionaires and dispossessed masses, I hope that this book's theme of hope will find a warm reception among many of us who are sorely tempted to despair. Moreover, I hope that these ancient biblical texts, with Brueggemann's magisterial expositions, will energize readers and spark imaginations in all who desire and are willing to work together toward an alternative and better organization of social life. Why should labor and production continue to serve the superrich? Why should human survival continue to depend on selling one's labor? Why shouldn't states serve those who are displaced, immiserated, infirmed, neglected, and abused? Why are so many regimes still organized around exploitation, inequality, and the devaluing of labor? The world we inhabit does not have to be the way that it is. May we never lose hope.

Special thanks to Stephanie, Miller, Nathaniel, Judy, Ron, and Vicki, who give me abundant reasons to hope. Everyone at Westminster John Knox, especially Julie Mullins, continues to delight me with patience, support, and helpful interventions. I'm not sure where I would be professionally without my many ongoing collaborations with Brennan Breed, but I surely am thankful for them, each and every one. Naming some neglects so many, but I want to mention a few people whose work continues to inspire and energize my thinking: Adam Kotsko, Adrian Johnston, Alenka Zupančič, Anna Kornbluh, Brent Strawn, Elaine James, Francis Landy, Joan Copjec, Joe Weiss, Rick Elmore, Sean Burt, Slavoj Žižek, Sylvie Honigman, Thomas Nail, Tim Beal, Tod Linafelt, Todd McGowan, and Yvonne Sherwood. I do not know every one of these folks personally, but each has personally impacted me profoundly. And once again, thank you to Walter Brueggemann, whose constant support is like an apple of gold in the silver setting of his unsurpassed brilliance, creativity, and energy.

Davis Hankins
Appalachian State University
June 15, 2022

PART ONE

Introducing Biblical Hope

Chapter 1

The Bible as Literature of Hope

The Jewish Bible, the Christian Old Testament, is fundamentally a literature of hope; yet, at least in Christian circles, the Old Testament has such a caricatured reputation as a tradition of law, judgment, and wrath. I want to explore this tradition of hope, as I judge it to be a very odd phenomenon, a problem in the Western tradition, and a great resource for our present cultural situation.

The Old Testament voices the oldest, deepest, most resilient grounding of hope in all human history, a hope that has been claimed by both Jews and Christians, but that is also operative beyond those traditions in more secular modes. The hope articulated in ancient Israel is not a vague optimism or a generic good idea about the future but a precise and concrete confidence in and expectation for the future that is rooted explicitly in YHWH's promises to Israel. In those promises, which are text specific, YHWH has sworn to effect futures of well-being that are beyond the present condition of the world and that cannot, in any credible way, be extrapolated from the present. The remarkable act of hope that permeates the Old Testament lies in the fact that the promises Israel heard and remembered link together the character and intent of YHWH, the creator of heaven and earth, with the concrete, material reality of the world. YHWH's promises characteristically do not concern escape from the world but transformation within it.

The dominant intellectual tradition of the West, that of Hellenistic philosophy, out of which has come the ground of reasonableness for science, is not a tradition of hope. It is a tradition of *order* that seeks to discern, understand, decipher, know, and, if possible, master and

3

control. Thus the biblical tradition lives in considerable tension with the dominant intellectual tradition and often has not had its full say. It is clear that *order* and *hope* are not about the same thing, nor are they easily held together. It is clear that both order and hope are essential for viable human community. We are in a season when the *urge for order* seems nearly to squeeze out the *voice of hope*. For that reason, for us to reflect on this tradition of hope is an important exercise.

Jews (and Christians after them) are a people of hope, but they can be a people of hope only if they are not alienated from and ignorant of their tradition. Therefore it is important to identify the shape and substance of that hope. In this chapter I will consider the main texts of hope, and in the next I will explore three major issues related to them.

Israel's hope is based on the character of YHWH, who utters promises and whose utterances Israel has found to be reliable. Indeed, the very nature of YHWH, as confessed by Israel, is to make promises and to watch over those promises to see that they come to fruition (see Josh. 21:43–45). Thus the Old Testament is an ongoing process of promise-making and promise-keeping. YHWH's promises tend to be clustered in four particular portions of the Old Testament text: the ancestral narratives, the covenant blessings in Leviticus and Deuteronomy, the prophets, and the Psalms. Furthermore, I begin by distinguishing seven elements of hope literature in the Bible, not all of equal power or significance. This catalog suggests how pervasive, even definitional, are the hope dimensions of this faith.

1. The ancestral narratives of Genesis 12–36 are replete with promises (a) that YHWH will give land to Israel and cause Israel to prosper in the land, where fertility is assured, and (b) that the nations will be blessed (see Gen. 12:1–3; 28:13–15). Von Rad and Westermann have established that the Genesis narratives are essentially narratives of hope.[1] The overriding substance of this literature is a promise from God that is open ended in its scope and definitions and is brought to fulfillment only by the fidelity of God. The substance of the promise is variously an heir, a great name, a new land, a community of blessing among the nations.[2]

Alt has shown that the God disclosed in the Genesis narratives is a God who makes promises and who keeps them.[3] This God is not to be linked in any way with totemism or the primitive religions that the historians of religion and the structuralists consider. Paul Ricoeur has shown that from the very outset this God, unlike so many around, is not an abiding presence but a speaker of a new word who breaks open all that is settled, routine, and conventional.[4] This is a God of *kerygma*, of a message that transforms reality.

The most dramatic examples of this powerful promise are related to Abraham. In Genesis 12:1–3 Abraham is summoned by this speaker of promise to leave his natural habitat and to go in naked trust to a different place, a place not even yet identified.[5] In 18:1–15 it is asserted, by means of a rhetorical question, that nothing is impossible for God.[6] It is promised that this God has the power to make things new by his promise, so new that birth displaces the long-standing and hopeless barrenness of Sarah and Abraham. The stories are not magical or supernatural in any conventional sense. Rather, they are recitals of the memory of the inexplicable happenings that have gone on in this family of hope. One can see how such memories enable this community to hope against all data and to believe that the *hopelessness* of the data never rules out a different *possibility*. God can indeed work a newness against all of the data. God can shatter the known world in order to establish a new historical possibility. Jews and Christians cling to such an affirmation.

Israel is portrayed as a people who sometimes doubt and resist this wonder of God, but on the whole, Israel in these narratives is ready to receive the word, trust the promise, and act in hope. Indeed, Israel's history in these early tales consists in responding to such impossible words and being willing to depart the known world on the basis of such a summons. That is what we have meant by a recital of "God's mighty deeds." In these tales the central dynamic of biblical faith is established. In the very character of God there is a push and an impetus to violate, overthrow, and depart the established order for the sake of a newness not yet comprehended or in hand.

2. The promises take a different form in the covenant blessings related to the Sinai traditions (Lev. 26:3–13; Deut. 28:1–14). Unlike the promises of Genesis, the blessings are part of a quid pro quo arrangement, so that the promises to Israel are assured when Israel obeys the commandments. In this tradition, the commands are the condition of hope.

3. The prophetic texts of the eighth to sixth century BCE, in lyrical promise passages, state the themes of promise, hope, and trust even

more baldly.[7] The prophetic promises look beyond the present and anticipate a new arrangement of the world "in the days to come." Here they are not encased in old narratives; they are poems that have no intent other than to tell the story of the future. These promises are not predictions but are rather acts of faithful imagination that dare to anticipate new futures on the basis of what YHWH has done in the past. They characteristically begin with "Behold, the days are coming," or "In that day." This rhetorical pattern affirms that there will be a day of turn in which the dominant order of things as we have known it will be terminated. God has no final commitment to the present ordering of things, which will be drastically displaced by a wholly new order. The new order is not at all to be established by human plan, human knowledge, or human power. It is the inscrutable, irresistible work of God. Again, as in the Genesis stories, the push and impetus come only from the mystery of God and from nowhere else.

The themes of prophetic hope are fairly constant. There is nothing here that is private, spiritual, romantic, or otherworldly. It is always social, historical, this-worldly, political, economic. The dream of God and the hope of Israel are for the establishment of a new social order that will embody peace, justice, freedom, equity, and well-being. Thus, not only is the tradition formally hope filled, but also the substance of that hope is clear. In some ways the substance of the hope as *a new social world* is even more radical than the formal claim of promise itself.

While the promises occur at various places in the prophetic literature, they are particularly clustered in the exilic materials, such as Isaiah 40–55, Jeremiah 30–33, and Ezekiel 33–48. We may cite from those as well as other examples of these prophetic visions.

(a) Perhaps the best known is the vision of peace in Micah 4:1–5, which for the most part is reiterated in Isaiah 2:1–5.[8] Its phrasing is well known:

> [T]hey shall beat their swords into plowshares
>   and their spears into pruning hooks;
> nation shall not lift up sword against nation,
>   neither shall they learn war any more.
>   Mic. 4:3

Micah then adds a shrewd economic note from the perspective of the peasant community (which is not in the Isaiah parallel) about the cost of such anticipated disarmament:[9]

> [T]hey shall all sit under their own vines and under their own
>   fig trees,
> and no one shall make them afraid.
>
> v. 4

The poet recognizes that serious disarmament requires a lowered standard of living, so that rapacious greed ends, taxes can be reduced, and people are satisfied with a little, just a vine and a fig tree. Yet they are in safety and well-being. The poem is an incredible act of hope. One cannot see how one can get from here to there, either in the ancient world or in our own time, but such hope is precisely a "conviction of things not seen" (Heb. 11:1).

(b) A second, very different promise is found in Isaiah 19:23–25.[10] It is the most sweeping geopolitical assertion in the Old Testament and can be heard in all its radicalness if one listens with an ear to the present situation in the same geographical locus:

> On that day there will be a highway from Egypt to Assyria, and the Assyrian will come into Egypt, and the Egyptian into Assyria, and the Egyptians will worship with the Assyrians.
> On that day Israel will be the third with Egypt and Assyria, a blessing in the midst of the earth, whom the LORD of hosts has blessed, saying, "Blessed be Egypt my people, and Assyria the work of my hands, and Israel my heritage."

In this remarkable vision the poet takes the words properly applied only to beloved Israel, words like "my people" and "work of my hands," and applies them to other nations that are in fact enemies.

The dream is for a time when the barriers of fear, insecurity, and inequality have been overcome, when there is free access among the nations who are traditional enemies. Again the hope of biblical faith is incredible, for one cannot see, among ancient empires or among contemporary nation-states, how this can come about. But Israel at its best, when informed by its memory, lives toward a vision that is as certain as is God's own word (cf. Isa. 55:10–11).

(c) In a very different idiom is the vision of Ezekiel 34:25–31:

> I will make with them a covenant of peace and banish wild ani-
> mals from the land, so that they may live . . . securely. . . . The
> trees of the field shall yield their fruit, and the earth shall yield its
> increase. They shall be secure on their soil; and they shall know
> that I am the LORD, when I break the bars of their yoke, and save
> them from the hands of those who enslaved them. . . . You are
> my sheep, the sheep of my pasture, and I am your God, says the
> Lord GOD.

This is a promise of a covenant of *shalom*, of well-being and prosperity. The promise moves in two rather remarkable directions. On the
one hand, it has a hope for the restoration of creation, the renewal of
the ecological process, so that the field and the earth will bring forth
abundantly. On the other hand, this renewal has a political compo-
nent. The banishment of "wild animals" may be read literally or as a
metaphor for rapacious political power. The breaking of "the yoke"
means an end to oppression. The promise thus articulates restoration
for both history and nature, for both politics and fertility, in which all
relationships will be as they were envisioned in the uncontaminated
anticipation of the creation narrative of Genesis 1.

(d) Finally, the promise of Isaiah 65:17–25 is the most sweeping
of the prophetic promises I will mention. It begins with these words
(vv. 17–18):

> For I am about to create new heavens
>   and a new earth;
> and the former things shall not be remembered
>   or come to mind.
> But be glad and rejoice forever
>   in what I am creating;
> for I am about to create Jerusalem as a joy,
>   and its people as a delight.

As the promise continues, the new heaven and new earth are characterized by a new economic order in which none will usurp the produce of others, by a new order of health without death in childbirth
and with no infant mortality, and by a new understanding with God
such that God shall be present and available at every point of need.
This poet has dreamed the most undisciplined, liberated vision of
them all. The prophets are resolute and unanimous. The way it is,

is not the way it will be. It is promised that there will be a decisive change in the shape of human life on earth.

4. In the Psalms we may identify two rhetorical practices of hope. First, in the great psalms of enthronement (Pss. 93; 95–99), the coming rule of YHWH is celebrated and welcomed by all creation:

> Let the heavens be glad, and let the earth rejoice;
>   let the sea roar, and all that fills it;
>   let the field exult, and everything in it.
> Then shall all the trees of the forest sing for joy
>   before the LORD; for he is coming,
>   for he is coming to judge the earth.
> He will judge the world with righteousness,
>   and the peoples with his truth.
> > Ps. 96:11–13

This large public doxology is matched by the second rhetorical practice, a much more intimate practice of faith in which individual Israelites voice complete hope for the future because of their unqualified confidence in YHWH:

> The LORD is my light and my salvation;
>   whom shall I fear?
> The LORD is the stronghold of my life;
>   of whom shall I be afraid?
> > Ps. 27:1; see 30:4–5

All these texts and their various images attest to Israel's conviction that YHWH has promised and intends to enact a new well-being for Israel and the world. YHWH's promise characteristically concerns peace, security, prosperity, fruitfulness, righteousness, and justice, which will come in the earth, not because of any claim the earth has, but because the one who utters promises in the hearing of Israel is the creator of heaven and earth, who is known in Israel to be reliable. Thus in the wondrous promises of Isaiah 2:2–4, Isaiah 11:1–9, and Micah 4:1–4, YHWH promises that the present earth will be healed by YHWH's own fidelity. Israel is therefore certain that YHWH will overcome every impediment and defeat every resistance to the well-being that YHWH intends for the world.

As the Old Testament develops, Israel's hope in YHWH is verbalized in two particular ways. On the one hand, Old Testament faith is *messianic*, believing that YHWH will dispatch and empower a particular human agent who will enact the new age that YHWH has promised. Thus, hope is "this-worldly," inside the present ordering of creation. On the other hand, Old Testament faith also developed in an *apocalyptic* mode, a cataclysmic hope that YHWH will effect YHWH's new world without any human agency. Despite their differences, both traditions attest to the coming "rule of YHWH" in which all creation will be ordered for YHWH's intent of peace, security, and justice. The later traditions of the Old Testament do not choose between these modes of faith, but hold them together in tension.

5. The great prophetic hopes are pushed one step further later in the faith of Israel as prophecy becomes apocalyptic.[11] Apocalyptic is the most extreme form of hope in the Bible, and the most misunderstood. Some do not understand that this is poetic imagination and instead want it to be a hard prediction to be assessed in detail. Such a view misunderstands both the character of the literature and the nature of hope in the Bible. The biblical way of hope is to dream large dreams about the powerful purposes of God, but they are not designs, blueprints, or programs. To make them such is to deny God's free governance over the future.

Apocalyptic literature is not pervasive in the Old Testament, but it flourishes in the period between the testaments.[12] Zechariah 14:8–9 offers a characteristic hope for Israel:

> On that day living waters shall flow out from Jerusalem, half of them to the eastern sea and half of them to the western sea; it shall continue in summer as in winter.
>   And the LORD will become king over all the earth; on that day the LORD will be one and his name one.

This imagery is so radical that it is pushed outside the historical process. In this anticipation the waters of life flow like the rivers of life in Genesis 2, but now the source is the holy temple city. The great vision is that YHWH, the God of Israel, will rule the nations. This hope is not unlike prophetic hope, except it is more extreme and has become cosmic. The canvas for Israel's hope cannot be contained or domesticated within the historical process. It must be as comprehensive as the lordly splendor of YHWH.

6. In both prophetic and apocalyptic texts we are presented with the overarching metaphor of biblical faith, namely, the kingdom of God, the rule of God, the ordering of life according to the purpose and will of God.[13] This hoped-for kingdom when God's will is fully visible will displace all the orderings and kingdoms of life that now claim our allegiance (Rev. 11:15).[14] The metaphor of the kingdom is a radical, revolutionary metaphor that stands in judgment over all the power arrangements presently available. The promised kingdom places all current arrangements in jeopardy. The coming of the new age and the new governance of God is at the heart of biblical faith. It has roots in the Sinai covenant, which Buber has seen to be a radical political assertion. It is the overriding context of the prophets, who expect and insist that God's rule take public and visible form. The metaphor comes to its most poignant expression in the tradition around Jesus. His life and teachings embody that rule of God, evident in his teachings (Mark 1:14–15), in his acts (Luke 7:21–23), and in his parables. In response to this massive tradition of hope, the church prays regularly that God's kingdom come on earth, as in heaven.[15]

7. Finally, of the dimensions of biblical hope I will mention, both Jews and Christians wait for the *Messiah who is to come.* Too much time has been wasted on Jewish–Christian conflicts over this hope.[16] What matters is that Jews and Christians hold firmly to the conviction that one will come from God who will "mend the world." How and when and who that will be is not a proper issue for these convictions of hope. For the theme of hope, it does not matter greatly that Jews wait for a first coming and Christians wait for a second coming. Jews and Christians stand waiting together.

At the center of that common faith is a contrast with the nonbelieving world. That world does not wait for the Messiah but for Godot, who never comes. Against such despair these convictions of faith know about a coming one who precludes resignation and despair. Indeed, the worship and theology informed by these convictions are largely a reflection on that staggering concrete act of hope. That hope is a reading of history against the common reading that leads to hopelessness. But, because God oversees history, it is affirmed that present shapes of reality and power are all provisional, kept open for the other One, not yet here but very sure to come.

Israel's capacity to trust these promises of YHWH is the substance of faith. Trust in YHWH's promises is not a particularly "religious" undertaking, but rather concerns living differently in the world. As the Old Testament looks beyond itself to what YHWH will yet do, that powerful expectation for God has been addressed variously by Jewish and by Christian interpretive traditions. No single tradition has a monopoly on the promises of YHWH, and no single tradition is the designated custodian of hope.

This catalog of biblical texts shows that hope belongs centrally and decisively to biblical faith. There is no way around it, if one takes the Bible seriously. These faith communities of Christians and Jews live in a passionate and profound hope that the world will become the world God intends, the world for which we yearn.

Viewed from the perspective of the dominant (and dominating) operating assumptions of our cultural context, the massive statement of hope contained in these texts seems foolish or, if not foolish, at best irrelevant. That is, it doesn't seem to touch the "real world," which appears so permanent. The promises belong to a different rationality and are presented precisely by poets and storytellers who operated (from our modern perspective) with a quite doubtful epistemology.

The dissonance in the juxtaposition of hope and reason needs to be taken seriously by us. The tradition of hope (Jewish-Christian faith) does not stand next to the tradition of reason (and science) in a chronological way, as though the hope tradition is primitive and has been superseded with the coming of modern knowledge. Nor is it the case that the tradition of hope can be bracketed out in a corner somewhere, as if it were a private religious mode separated off from the great public questions of power. The hope tradition is alive and addresses the realities of public life. It moves with an alternative reason of a different sort, which might be called "historical reason."[17]

The issue of the juxtaposition of hope and knowledge is at the heart of the crisis now to be faced in our culture. The traditions of *scientific knowledge and power* seem oddly alienated from the traditions of hope.[18] The tradition of hope means a relinquishment of control over life, not in the sense of life being out of control, but in the sense of governance being entrusted to this Holy One whom we cannot explain. This hope does not consist of losing control, but relinquishing it in trust.[19] It is thus an important question in our society about what happens if the managers of scientific knowledge can no longer entertain serious, concrete hope beyond our knowledge. Under such conditions, control becomes defensive and perhaps oppressive. The tradition of hope has its powerful say now among those cut off from scientific power and alienated by scientific norms of context. *The substance of biblical hope*, reflected in these texts, is a new world of justice, equity, freedom, and well-being. This hope has nothing to do with progress, for what is promised is wrought in inscrutable ways by the gift of the holy God where we least expect it.[20]

A strong case has been made that a defining mark of a postindustrial, technological world is despair, the inability to trust in any new and good future that is promised and may yet be given. Insofar as despair marks the current social environment of faith, to that extent hope is a distinctive mark of faith with dangerous and revolutionary social potential.

Questions for Reflection

1. *Kerygma* is a message that transforms reality. As you explore our current realities, what do you witness as needing transformative change? What needs to be made new in your life, your community, the world?

2. Brueggemann calls the prophetic promises "acts of faithful imagination" that will usher the vision of God anew into our own spaces and contexts. Often our own imaginations may limit us in our work toward transformation. What is hindering your imagination? How are you opening yourself up to the imagination and creativity of God?

3. The hopes found in the Bible, from prophecy to apocalyptic texts, are vast and varied as characters experience life and suffer because of oppressive institutions and war. The prophets spoke both in terms of help to come in this world, through the human agency of a messiah, and imagining a final cosmic restoration. Where do you fall on this spectrum of hope, in our current context?

4. There can be a fraught tension between the concept of hope and the dire realities that the traditions of reason and scientific knowledge point toward. It can be difficult to look for signs of hope when we so often experience the polarized extremes of willful ignorance on the

one hand and doomsday portrayals on the other concerning issues like climate change or gun violence. In the midst of realities like this, how do you encounter the "biblical hope" Brueggemann describes, of giving over a sense of control to a God who can be trusted to bring about a new order of things?

Chapter 2

Living toward a Vision

The biblical texts of hope cited in the previous chapter announce that a better world of justice and equity is coming, as promised by God. Yet this tradition of hope raises several issues, such as: What is the function of hope? Why is hope practiced? What happens when a people hopes? The answer I make is, *Hope keeps the present arrangement open and provisional.* Hope reminds us that the way things are (and all the extrapolations we make from that), is precarious and in jeopardy. Hope reminds us not to absolutize the present, not to take it too seriously, not to treat it too honorably, because it will not last.

I

Because hope has such a revolutionary function, it is more likely that failure to hope—hopelessness—happens among the affluent, the prosperous, the successful, the employable, the competent, for whom the present system works so well. We are the ones who are likely to be seduced into taking the present political, economic, intellectual system too seriously and equating it with reality. Indeed, it is prudent to take it that way, because that is where the jobs and benefits are. The more one benefits from the rewards of the system, the more one is enraptured with the system, until it feels like the only game in town and the whole game. Our "well-offness" leads us finally to absolutize, so that we may say that "the system is the solution." The system wants us to believe that, for such belief silences criticism. It

15

makes us consenting, docile, obedient adults. The system wants to contain all our hopes and fears, wants us to settle for the available system of rewards.

We may say of the system's claim to absolutism, first, that the system does not comprehend and benefit everyone and everything. There are always outsiders who are excommunicated and nullified and declared nonexistent. Every political system serves some at the cost of others. Every economic system benefits some at the expense of others. Every intellectual system eliminates the data and the people who do not fit. The urgent, unavoidable question then is, *What about those others?* What about the ones without access? Do they count? Are they bad? Are they nonpersons? We have a long history of denying the existence of those who are poor, women, Black people, people who have a disability, all kinds of disqualified people. The more rigorously the absolutizing works, the tighter they are locked out, and the more of them there are who are locked out.

Second, biblical faith is suspicious of the system. It suggests that even those well inside the system should not expect too much. That is, even for its own adherents, the system finally cannot keep all its promises. So it is with the phone company; to say that the phone company is the solution to communications is surely not true, because communication is a human possibility and a human problem. This is not to say that the phone company has no value, but simply that systems in their hopelessness tend to make pretentious claims and run roughshod over those who doubt or resist. Such pretentious claims pushed to extremity become idolatry.

So what is the function of hope of this unreasonable, exotic kind? It is to provide standing ground *outside the system* from which the system can be evaluated, critiqued, and perhaps changed. Hopeless people eventually must conform, but hope-filled people are not as dependent, not as fully contained and administered. Hope is an immense human act that reminds us that no system of power or knowledge can finally grasp what is true. We must take care not to surrender our imaginative power to any pretension of absoluteness. Let me cite three examples of this critical function of hope.

1. The text of Isaiah 55:1–5 is set in the sixth-century exile, when Jews were contained in the brutal Babylonian system of reality. Babylonian religion (Isa. 46) and Babylonian politics (Isa. 47) had

largely claimed the day. In this context the Israelite poet issues an incredibly promissory statement:

> Ho, everyone who thirsts,
>   come to the waters;
> and you that have no money,
>   come, buy and eat!
> Come, buy wine and milk
>   without money and without price.
> Why do you spend your money for that which is not bread,
>   and your labor for that which does not satisfy?
>
> Isa. 55:1–2

The poet sets up a contrast between the "work bread" system of the empire and the "free food" system of the Israelite God. It is the memory of manna, of strangely given bread for the destitute, that becomes the ground of hope (see Exod. 16). This is not the offer of a production scheme, only an imaginative act of hope wrought in poetry. The poet lives toward a vision and dares to think about a time to come when there will be no hunger, because bread will be given for all.[1] It is a fanciful, visionary assertion, the kind out of which new history is wrought.

Notice what this poem does. It permits a critique to be announced. The poetry is addressed to those without hope who had accepted Babylonian definitions of reality, who thought all life was reduced to a single Babylonian definition. The poet invites Israelites to disengage their imagination from Babylonian shapes of reality. In fact, this poetry amounts to a delegitimation of Babylonian authority.[2] The power of poetic hope creates a way in which Israelites may have freedom of action, but the freedom of action apart from the all-consuming system depends on the *freedom of imagination* and speech done by the poet.[3] The hope of a different bread system permits and authorizes a critique of the empire.

2. In Isaiah 65:17–25 the promissory vision of new heaven and new earth is an act of critical hope. This text is an eloquent statement of an alternative reality that is the substance of hope. It is the literature of a disenfranchised community that was oppressed by the dominant priesthood.[4] That priesthood so controlled and preempted everything in terms of power, influence, and access that the minority

group speaking in this poetry had its life nearly squeezed out. Isaiah 65 is the poetry of that minority that asserts an alternative mode of historical existence.

It is in a situation of marginality that the poet speaks. This act of hope, I submit, is to be taken not literally but poetically. The poem wants the oppressed group to have freedom of space and courage enough to act. Yet it could not do so as long as the absolute present prevailed. As long as the dominant group controlled everything, no one had power to act against it. This vision of new heaven, new earth, and new Jerusalem, however, invites the hopeless to act in a fresh way.

3. The third example occurs in the book of Daniel. The book of Daniel is filled with extravagant hope against the tight system of royal reality. The symbol of oppressive political power is King Nebuchadnezzar, who may be taken to refer to any oppressive power.[5] That is, Nebuchadnezzar is symbol and model, not a historical person. He is presented as the paradigm of all totalitarian evil. In the narrative of 3:16–18 Nebuchadnezzar wants these model Jewish men, Shadrach, Meshach, and Abednego, to bow down. That is, he wants them to acknowledge the absolute claims of the imperial system, to concede the absolute authority of the system over their lives. These three Jews, though, are model practitioners of hope. They are so grounded in the liberation tradition of hope that they will not finally submit. They believe there is a future yet to be given that is not under the control of the king. The fact that their lives are grounded in the hope of a future given by God makes it possible for them to defy the system of Nebuchadnezzar. Out of their hope they offer this marvelous syllogism:

> O Nebuchadnezzar, we have no need to present a defense to you in this matter. If our God whom we serve is able to deliver us from the furnace of blazing fire and out of your hand, O king, let him deliver us. But if not, be it known to you, O king, that we will not serve your gods and we will not worship the golden statue that you have set up. (Dan. 3:16–18)

Their hope is a wonderful act of defiance. Perhaps we will be delivered. Perhaps not. Either way, we will not submit. Hope makes it possible not to submit. No wonder the response of the men fills the king with fury (Dan. 3:19): it signifies a dramatic end of his royal claims and his capacity to intimidate.

In all three cases—Isaiah 55 in exile against Babylon, Isaiah 65 against an oppressive priesthood, and Daniel 3 against Nebuchadnezzar—hope gives reason not to submit to present power arrangements. Hope affirms, in each case, that the present well-established power is not permanent and need not be taken with too much seriousness.

Herbert Schneidau has written an important book on Israel's historical perspective. His book's telling title, *Sacred Discontent*, precisely captures Israel's perspective.[6] Israel has a chronic discontent with the present. It is endlessly suspicious and refuses to accept the orders of the day. Schneidau labels this discontent "sacred" because it comes of God. This "sacred discontent" is rooted in *hope*. The hope is in the overriding power of God to work a new will against the order of the day. It is this act of hope that holds the present critically and loosely. Israel knows, in all these texts, that the purpose of God finally will move against the way things are. The function of this sacred discontent that is Israel's hope is to keep us from becoming excessively contented with the way things are.

II

The second issue emerging from these biblical texts of hope is, What is the *normal habitat of hope?* Who keeps the present open to new interventions from God, and in what contexts? The hope tradition in ancient Israel suggests this answer: *hope emerges among those who publicly articulate and process their grief over their suffering.* That answer is an oddity, but it is more than an oddity. It is a great mystery that cuts to the heart of biblical faith. It is a fact of experience that violates all of our reasonable expectations. We would not expect hope to emerge especially and peculiarly among the ones who suffer.

At the outset, let us identify three places where hope is unlikely to appear with any power. First and most surprising, hope does not appear among the managers of the status quo. They may be optimists or progressives or evolutionists or developmentalists, but they are not the most likely to be ones who hope. People excessively committed to present power arrangements and present canons of knowledge tend not to wait expectantly for the newness of God.

In the historical narrative of Israel we may see this reality among the kings and priests, the managers of the status quo. Regularly these leaders are juxtaposed to the prophets, who are the voices of hope in Israel. The prophets intend that priests and kings should listen and be open to the risk of the future, but characteristically they do not do so. Characteristically priests and kings seek to silence prophets and crush the voice of hope, because they find this voice too threatening. We may cite King Ahab, who regarded Elijah as a "troubler" (1 Kgs. 18:17). We may refer to Amaziah, the royal priest who banished the prophet Amos (Amos 7:10–17). We may observe the kings and governors a century later who wanted to execute Jeremiah (Jer. 26, 36) because he spoke a critical word that opened the present to the surprise of the future.

The reaction of those in control to such a critical word of hope is to become defensive, to attempt to keep the future from impinging on the present in any serious way. Jeremiah (6:14; 8:11) sees this manipulative ploy. They say, "*Shalom, shalom,* well-being, well-being, peace and prosperity," when things are in fact not like that at all. Ezekiel (13:8–16) accuses the managers of the status quo of "whitewash," of covering over the incongruities and attempting to keep the system intact, even when that system has ceased to function. The managers (be they kings, priests, or false prophets) do not wait or expect or anticipate, because they believe that whatever comes next will be a diminishment of what they have now. Such people become adept at labels, crying "treason" (Jer. 38:4), "conspirator" (Amos 7:10), or "blasphemer" (Mark 2:7) against any who hope against the present. Finally, those who are excessively limited to the present ordering of things are hopeless.

Second and closely related, hope does not appear among the intellectuals who reflect on systems categories and expect nothing new from God. We might call this group statespersons, advisors, or even consultants. Their task in ancient Israel is to reflect on how things work, to make things work for their patrons.[7] These intellectuals think, shrewd as they are, in a closed, managed system. That system is clearly discernible in the book of Proverbs. Life is understood in terms of fixed cause-and-effect relationships. To be sure, life is not fully buttoned down, as there is always some inexplicable element, but the technical explanation of the inexplicable is the main point of such an intellectual enterprise.[8] It is the kind of knowledge a regime can live with and sponsor. Indeed, one would not expect in the book of Proverbs any radical statement of disruption, discontinuity, or hope. This sapiential outlook comes to its weary culmination in the book of Ecclesiastes, which concludes that there really is no new thing, no ground for hope:

> All streams run to the sea,
>   but the sea is not full;
> to the place where the streams flow,
>   there they continue to flow.
>   Eccl. 1:7

> What has been is what will be,
>   and what has been done is what will be done;
> there is nothing new under the sun.
>   v. 9

The present presumed world contains and accounts for everything.[9]

Third, hope does not appear among the oppressed silent sufferers. This argument is literally *an argument from silence*. That is, the people in bondage are so beaten down that they cannot utter a word. They cannot speak their hurt. They cannot articulate their grief and misery. I cite no texts, because these people give us no text. If we had a text for them, then they would have a voice. But they have no voice, so no text, and so no hope. That is why every totalitarian regime controls the media to keep others silent, stops the artists, and forbids assembly. People become dangerous voices of hope when they assemble or have a chance for solidarity, but if they can be kept mute, they can be held in servility.

Hope is not likely to come then among royal managers, among hired intellectuals, or among the muted oppressed. Who hopes? Those who enter their grief, suffering, and oppression, who bring it to speech, who publicly process it and move through it and beyond. They are the ones who are surprised to find, again and again, that hope and new social possibility come in the midst of such grief (see Rom. 5:3). Grief of that sort can be silenced from two sides, *from beneath* by those too beaten to cry and *from above* by those who see no pain.

The governing example of biblical hope is the exodus narrative. That event is the primal act of hope in the Bible. Out of it comes a certitude that God will sooner or later bring justice and freedom into the world, even for slaves, even against empires. That certitude, however, was not arrived at easily. It arose from the oppressed people around Moses who made bricks for the empire. In the face of Pharaoh this people groaned. They cried out. They protested. They raged. They brought their common misery to public speech, which must have been an incredibly dangerous thing to do. Such common misery brought to public speech is a force in history that neither the tyrannical Pharaoh nor the great God above can ignore. It is written in this story of hope that "God heard their groaning, and God remembered his covenant. . . . God looked upon the Israelites, and God took notice of them" (Exod. 2:24–25). Suffering brought to speech concerns hope, because such protest in prayer and in public life is a refusal to let things be this way when they are in fact unbearable.

Out of that model event and that modeling narrative, we may extrapolate to our own time. The serious new hope for traditionally marginalized and underrepresented groups in our time has come from *pain expressed*. It could come no other way. It was the long experience of pain and grief voiced that led to Martin Luther King Jr.'s "I have a dream." It was the sisterhood come to voice that brought hope to many depressed and immobilized women. It is complaint made visible that led to greater accessibility and visibility of people with diverse abilities and disabilities. Indeed, if there is no grief brought to voice, there will be only status quo, only hopelessness, only invisibility, and therefore docility.

III

The third issue emerging from these biblical texts of hope is, Who are *the enemies of hope*? What works to keep hope from having power among us? I will suggest three aspects of an answer, which I judge to be clearly biblical and also clearly urgent in our contemporary scene.

1. The first enemy of hope is *silence, civility, and repression.*[10] Where grief is denied and suffering is kept isolated, unexpressed, and unprocessed in a community, we may be sure hopelessness will follow. Silence may come because this sufferer lacks the courage or will to speak. But behind that, I submit, is *the long-term pressure from above.* The rulers of this age crave order above all. They have learned that silence is the way to preserve order, even if that order is unjust and dysfunctional. Where there is no speech about grief and suffering, there can be no hope.

In the New Testament, in Mark 10:46–52, there is a remarkable incident concerning the blind beggar Bartimaeus. He waited along the road. When he heard that Jesus was coming, he began to cry out for help. He said, "Have mercy on me." He understood well the injunction "Ask, and it will be given." He asked in the only way he knew how. The next line in the narrative is most surprising: "Many sternly ordered him to be quiet." Do you wonder why? Because it was an embarrassment, a disruption, just not nice? Perhaps so. Or perhaps that is the only way one can administer beggars. If he were kept silent, he would remain hopeless and remain a docile beggar, but the narrative goes on to say, "He cried out even more loudly." He was not muted and therefore not hopeless. By the end of the story he has gained well-being, but he had to resist the pressure to be silent, or he would have had no chance, no hope.

2. On the other side, the great enemy of hope is *fulfillment.* Scholars call this "realized eschatology." Good news tempts people to imagine that the promises are fully kept and the gifts already actualized. Thus, for example, Paul rebukes the Corinthians for their arrogance in presuming that their existence is the complete fulfillment of God's promise (1 Cor. 4:8). If *muteness* is a problem from below, obviously *fulfillment* is a problem from above, from the well-off who are satiated to boredom and cynicism, who have no want, desire nothing, and need only to protect what they already have. The narcotic power of fulfillment is evident in the parable of Luke 12:16–21 (cf. 1 Kgs. 4:20–21). "The land of a rich man produced abundantly." The line is overloaded with blessing. The man had *land.* It was bottomland. He had a good crop. He could think only of storing the blessing. He said, "You have ample goods laid up for many years; relax, eat, drink, be merry." Abruptly he dies, prematurely. He dies,

says the story, because he was poor toward God. When the present is coterminous with our best dreams, then there is no further dream, no vision toward which to live, and finally no hope.

3. I am so bold as to suggest that the third enemy of hope is *technique*, the capacity to figure out, analyze, and problem solve. I understand that people of hope cannot live without technique. For that reason, the relationship between hope and technique is a delicate and complex problem, and I do not oversimplify. But, because my theme is hope, I am driven to consider the ways in which technique may nullify hope. In the Bible, technique, the capacity to reduce life's mysteries to manageable, discrete elements, is embodied in the wise men of Pharaoh (Exod. 8), who are called magicians; in the wise men and magicians in the Joseph narrative (Gen. 41), who are to interpret dreams; in the wise men of Nebuchadnezzar, who fail (Dan. 2); and in the religious experts who are condemned (Deut. 18:9–11), who manage the religious system. There may be other examples, but this is a fair sample. Notice the representatives of technique include both religious and secular political experts who believe that the data on hand, when rightly read, will provide sufficient knowledge and power to handle the future.

My comments in regard to hope and technique are not so much about knowledge as they are about a *sociology of knowledge*. That is, where do these technocrats live, how do they discern, and for whom? They tend to live in the patronage of the established order. Technique is never democratically distributed, nor is its use neutral. It is always funded and sponsored by the "big house," and so, predictably, it is likely to serve those ends. Not only are the wise funded by the established patronage, but also the knowledge so derived is always in the interest of royal policy. Technique is never disinterested. Its interest is to domesticate and harness the future for "reasons of state."

These narratives are in the Bible because in each instance the expert of technique fails, and an outsider must be brought in. In each case (Moses, Joseph, Daniel) the outsider turns out to be a faithful Israelite, one who has no credentials but is grounded in hope, and therefore has the capacity to gain life and give it. Perhaps the Bible means to be making something of an ironic statement on this subject to say that *the reality of power and knowledge* does not always cohere with *the forms of power and knowledge*. It is a question in Israel (and perhaps always) how the liberated power of hope and the careful administration of technique can live with each other.

IV

The power of hope in the biblical texts focuses on these three issues that must be faced if we are to understand hope as more than religious escapism:

1. The function of hope is to keep the present open and provisional, under scrutiny.
2. The natural setting of hope is among those who have grief and process it in the community.
3. The enemies of hope include muteness, fulfillment, and technique, all ways of trying to keep life on our own terms.

The capacity for hope is profoundly at issue in our society. Ours is a society in which hopelessness is prevalent and powerful. The power of hopelessness as a social force is extraordinary because the various enemies of hope are in a remarkable alliance. This includes these:

1. The mute servants (silent majority) who will never risk but always conform
2. The affluent who are satiated with fulfillment
3. The bright ones with technique who inevitably are sponsored by the royal house[11]

It is not fated that none of these should hope, but it is probable that none of these will hope. If that be so, then we are tempted into a deeper season of despair and hopelessness, reinforced both from above and from below. Despair does crazy things to us. The evidences of despair in our time include

the action of *terrorists*, which is a desperate, hopeless act of those without access or prospect of access to dignity or influence;

the posture of *conformity* among those who refuse to question
but are ready to embrace and salute whatever turns out to be
established official truth, both political and religious;
the temptation to *absolutize*, in which critical capacity is routinely impossible in public life.

Temptations to terror, conformity, and absolutizing are all a piece.
They breed in contexts where there is no prospect of a future that will
be different from the present.

Despair may be the critical fact of our common life. When we
despair, we do crazy, inhumane, and ruthless things in the world,
as is now widespread both publicly and domestically. This biblical
tradition of hope stands as an alternative, an invitation to practice a
critical dream, but that alternative requires a certain disengagement,
a certain risky imagination. The people gathered around the biblical
texts of hope practice that risky imagination from time to time. It
begins in not eating at the king's table (Dan. 1). Eating at the king's
table invites despair. An alternative diet of manna makes hope possible and powerful.

Questions for Reflection

1. As Brueggemann explains, the systems of our time want hope to fail,
    and they want us to be complicit in them, seduced by their benefits.
    But hope opens us to a new reality that beckons us beyond the sys-
    tem. How does hope open you up to see that the system is temporary,
    and how you benefit from it? Who is not benefiting?

2. Having hope means that we are able to use the "freedom of imagina-
    tion" to place ourselves outside of oppressive systems, so that we
    may stoke a "chronic discontent" with the present in order to move
    toward change. What is happening in your community? In what cre-
    ative ways might you imagine joining God's work to create more
    just systems?

3. The bearers of hope, as explained by Brueggemann, are the ones
    who cry out, protest, rage, and bring their common misery to public
    speech. Who are these bearers of hope right now in your life, in your
    community, in our society?

4. The great enemies of hope are silence, fulfillment, and technique—
   the ability to problem solve. Brueggemann goes into great detail
   about how these concepts stifle hope. Look within yourself. How
   are you being silent? In what ways are you content with the present,
   fulfilled with what you have benefited from? Ask yourself, who is
   creating and handling the data and narratives and knowledge that
   support the established order? How can marginalized people be
   empowered to create different sets of knowledge that might challenge the established order?

PART TWO

The Torah: Hope in Promises and Expectations

Chapter 3

The Open-Ended Hope of the Torah

*T*he Torah comprises the first five books of the Jewish and Christian Scriptures. In Christian usage the term "Torah" is characteristically mistranslated as "law" (based on the Greek *nomos*); it is better rendered as "instruction," that is, a teaching that gives guidance. In its final, canonical form, the Torah is the normative instruction of Judaism and, derivatively, the normative tradition to which Jesus and the early church regularly appeal. The Torah instruction is constituted by a combination of narrative and commandments, though it is not clear how the two relate to each other. A great deal of scholarly energy has been used in seeking to understand this relationship. Adele Berlin writes:

> Is the Torah a series of legal collections with narrative sections serving as the glue that holds them together, or is the Torah primarily a narrative, with some blocks of legal material inserted here and there? . . . Is the narrative the background for the laws or is the law a detail of the narrative? This is like asking whether in the perceptual puzzle the image is an urn or a human profile. In the Torah, there could be no set of laws without the narrative of revelation and no narrative of revelation without the laws. The laws would have no *raison d'être* without the revelation narrative

Editor's note: Some of the material in chapters 3, 5, 6, 7, and 8 appeared in a textbook on the Old Testament intended for use in introductory seminary classrooms, which is why parts of these chapters are written in a more didactic style and why Brueggemann is more attentive to the traditioning process that led to the formation of the biblical texts. As readers will see, Brueggemann's attention to these historical details results in theological insights that are characteristically profound.

and the revelation would have no content without the laws. While we need to continue to analyze individual laws and law collections, we also need to consider the possibilities of more profound meanings that the laws together with their narratives may evoke.[1]

Critical scholarship has spent long years of effort on the literary prehistory of the Torah, that is, the complicated traditioning processes that eventually arrived at the five scrolls that came to constitute the canonical, normative Torah. In sum, that phase of critical scholarship over a period of 250 years reached the conclusion that the Torah is constituted (a) by the use of a rich and complex variety of traditions that derive from many contexts (including ready appropriations from non-Israelite materials and cultures) and (b) by shaping and interpreting those materials, over time, through a steady, fairly constant theological intentionality. That is, the traditioning process is a sustained practice of *appropriation* and *transformation* of available materials. The outcome is a complex tradition, a product of an equally complex traditioning process that roughly—quite roughly—serves as an attestation to the character, purpose, and presence of YHWH, the God of Israel, who is the creator of heaven and earth and who is the deliverer and commander of Israel.

It is evident, however, that this steady interpretive resolve does not everywhere fully prevail in the text that became the Torah, so that the Torah itself reflects ongoing tension between a *variety of materials* that continue to have something of their own say and a *theological intentionality* that seeks to bring coherence to the complexity and variety of the materials and, where necessary, to override and trump the initial claims of extant materials. More critical study (to be found in the academy) attends primarily to the *complexity and variety* of the materials, whereas more focused "church interpretation" gives primary attention to the *theological constancy* produced by the canonical traditioning process. My judgment is that our reading must attend to both of these tasks and permit neither to silence or depreciate the other. It is clear to me, moreover, that neither of these perspectives is privileged as more intellectually respectable, so that the demanding part of responsible interpretation is to take seriously both the critical attentiveness to the variety and complexity and the "canonical" impetus toward constancy and coherence.

While there is more to say on this topic, here it is enough to recognize that the canon of the Torah, as the outcome of a complex and, in part, intentional traditioning process, has produced a normative text as the ground for faithful Jewish imagination and practice and, derivatively, for Christian imagination and practice as well. What counts is the way in which a relatively constant *theological intentionality* is woven through and eventually made intrinsic to the *complexity of materials*. It is clear that human agents have been at work through the entire traditioning process. They witness to the will, purpose, and presence of YHWH, who remains inscrutably hidden in and through the text and yet who discloses YHWH's own holy self through that same text.

I

It is a widespread assumption that the Torah reached roughly its final form by the time of the exile or soon thereafter (587–537 BCE). It is important to pause over the usage of "exile," which is not as simple as one might think.[2] The biblical narrative itself attests that the decisive leadership of the Jerusalem community was deported by the Babylonians away from Judah to distant areas in Babylon (see 2 Kgs. 24–25; Ps. 137; Jer. 52). There they remained an identifiable community with high self-regard (as in Jer. 24) until Cyrus the Persian ruler conquered Babylon and permitted a return of some Jewish exiles after 537 (see 2 Chr. 36:22–23). This notion of "exile" has been recently challenged on historical grounds, to suggest that the reality of deportation was less decisive and radical than the biblical record attests, that the notion of "exile" is an ideological term designed to establish the pedigree and assert the legitimacy of certain elements in the Jewish community as the proper leadership for the reconstitution of the community.

For our purposes it does not matter greatly if the exile is "historical," as given us in the Bible (as I am inclined to think), or if it is an ideological self-characterization. Either way, displaced people needed a place from which to validate a theologically informed, peculiar sense of identity and practice of life. The traditioning process that produced the Torah thus strikes me as a remarkable match for displacement, so that we may understand "the Torah of Moses" as a *script for displaced community*. It may be that the final form of the Torah was not reached in the brief period of the Babylonian displacement, but rather in the subsequent Persian period, during which there continued to be communities of passionate Jews far from Jerusalem. Either way, after the disruption of 587, under Babylonian or Persian aegis, Jews understood themselves to be exposed, vulnerable, and at risk, without the visible supports of a stable homeland.

So it is profoundly significant that the Torah of Moses concludes in Deuteronomy 34 with the death of Moses (thus the end of the normative period) and Israel poised to enter the land of promise but still landless. We may believe that this now-normative tradition was powerfully and peculiarly germane to a community that understood itself as exiles, poised to reenter the land but still landless. This community, seemingly without resources, asserted that this tradition was an adequate and reliable resource for its continuing life. It need hardly be said that the Torah has continued to be the primary resource for ongoing generations in the Jewish community that are characteristically displaced people at risk. Derivatively, the same claim for the Torah as primary resource is also true for Christians engaged in radical and serious obedience.

II

The Torah is then a normative resource, rooted in the authority of Moses, for the sustenance of a peculiar community of hope, faith, and life that is displaced and without other resources. The narrative traditioning process, propelled by great theological intentionality, was able, through great imaginative maneuvers, to fashion widely variegated and diffuse memories into a more or less coherent statement upon which this otherwise resourceless community could stake its life.

The Torah is thus a normative *act of hopeful imagination* that serves to sustain and legitimate a distinct community of gratitude and obedience. That distinct community, whether in the Assyrian, Babylonian, or Persian period, lived among cultural pressures and political powers that had no appreciation of its distinctiveness, no doubt found that distinctiveness at best an inconvenience, and, if possible, would have abrogated it. The risk and threat to this distinctive community in exile, however, was not primarily external pressure.

Much more likely the threat to the future of the community, with its peculiar wonder and its particular gratitude, was the internal reality that the world of Jewishness, sustained by an imaginative traditioning process, was too costly and demanding for some of its members. Thus the endless pressure of the easier option of dominant culture would eventually erode Jewishness. There is evidence that some in the community readily joined the dominant culture and became economically successful in doing so. We may anticipate, moreover, that some ended in despair, no longer able to make the courageous interpretive connection from remembered wonder to anticipated wonder. Thus we may imagine that the sustained community of Jews who held to the tradition without compromise was a small, disciplined, intentional group—perhaps elite in learning or authority or economics or all of the above—who became the nucleus of emerging Judaism. Even that minority, however, could not have been sustained without this tradition of normative miracles and disciplines of command, so that we may conclude that the Torah is the God-given strategy through which a faithful community at risk is sustained.

If the requirements of exile were costly and demanding for adults who went deep into memory and so sustained hope (see Lam. 3:21–24), we may imagine that the *transmission to the next generation* of this radical, buoyant distinctiveness was urgent and deeply problematic. The young, who did not after a while remember the ancient glories of Israel, were surely candidates for membership in the dominant culture of the empire, at the expense of this distinctiveness. It is likely that the Torah is peculiarly aimed at the young, in order to invite them into this distinct identity of wonder, gratitude, and obedience.

We may notice two uses that suggest this intergenerational crisis to which the community attended.

In Exodus 12–13 there is a pause in the narrative in order to provide detailed guidance for the celebration of the Passover that will remember the exodus as here narrated. It is curious that in the very telling of this defining wonder of deliverance, the tradition pauses in that telling to provide for subsequent celebrations. It is, moreover, noteworthy that while Christians tend to glide over these two chapters of instruction easily and quickly, Jewish readers give primary attention to this material of instruction, for it is the repeated celebration of the memory of the exodus that sustains Jewish identity when it is under threat from a dominant culture.[3] One suspects that the tradition pauses for so long and goes into such detail about celebration because the inculcation of the young was urgent and could not wait, not even until the end of the narrative of deliverance. The instruction, in its final form, aims at the young in exile who may be ready to turn away from the community into dominant culture. Thus "Moses" three times focuses precisely on the children:

> And when your children ask you, "What do you mean by this observance?" you shall say, "It is the passover sacrifice to the LORD, for he passed over the houses of the Israelites in Egypt, when he struck down the Egyptians but spared our houses." (Exod. 12:26–27)

> You shall tell your child on that day, "It is because of what the LORD did for me when I came out of Egypt." It shall serve for you as a sign on your hand and as a reminder on your forehead, so that the teaching of the LORD may be on your lips; for with a strong hand the LORD brought you out of Egypt. (13:8–9)

> When in the future your child asks you, "What does this mean?" you shall answer, "By strength of hand the LORD brought us out of Egypt, from the house of slavery. When Pharaoh stubbornly refused to let us go, the LORD killed all the firstborn in the land of Egypt, from human firstborn to the firstborn of animals." (13:14–15)

The question asked by the child is highly stylized, as in contemporary Passover celebrations. Behind this stylization, however, the child may be ignorant and unaware and really want to know; or perhaps the question is posed skeptically and defiantly. Either way, the normative tradition provides what is meant to be a compelling response to the child.

In parallel fashion, the tradition of Deuteronomy aims to recruit the young into a distinct lore of wonder and a distinctive discipline of gratitude that issues in visible obedience.[4]

When your children ask you in time to come, "What is the meaning of the decrees and the statutes and the ordinances that the LORD
our God has commanded you?" then you shall say to your children, "We were Pharaoh's slaves in Egypt, but the LORD brought
us out of Egypt with a mighty hand." (Deut. 6:20–21)

Thus the Torah provides the materials for the social construc-
tion of reality and for socialization of the young into *an alternative
world* where YHWH lives and governs. I cannot overstate that the
Torah, in its final, normative form, is an act of faithful imagination
that buoyantly and defiantly mediates a counterworld that is a wondrous, demanding alternative to the world immediately and visibly at
hand. The world visibly and immediately at hand is characteristically
a world that has no patience with Jews or with the God of the Jews,
that has no tolerance for wonder when the world can be managed,
no appreciation for gratitude when the world can be taken in self-
sufficiency, and certainly no readiness for obedience when the world
is known to be an arena for autonomy.

While we Christians are accustomed in Western Christendom to
take the Bible as the ultimate source of our given world, the Torah is
recurringly a contradiction of the world we regularly regard as given.
It was so in the ancient world of hostile powers with their cultural
hegemony where social givenness resisted the rule of YHWH. It is,
moreover, surely so in the modern world of Enlightenment rationality or in the postmodern world of fragmentation and its privatization
of meaning.

It has been a characteristic task of Jewish teaching, nurture, and
socialization to invite the young into the world of miracle, and so
to resist assimilation. Only of late have alert Christians in Euro-
American contexts noticed that the challenge that has always been
before Jews is now a fresh challenge for Christians as well. As the
Western world has been perennially hostile to the claims of Jewish faith, so the emerging contemporary world of commodity grows
more signally hostile to the claims of Christian faith as well. As has
not been the case in the long Christian hegemony of the West, now
the church is having to think and act to maintain a distinct identity
for faith in an alien cultural environment. While the church will characteristically attend to the New Testament in such an emergency, a

study of the Torah already alerts us to the resources for this crisis that are older and deeper than the New Testament.

The Jews in exile reported themselves dismayed about singing the songs of Zion in a strange land (Ps. 137:1–3). Now Christians face that same issue. The liberal Christian temptation is to accommodate dominant culture until faith despairs. The conservative Christian temptation is to fashion an absoluteness that stands disconnected from the dominant culture. Neither of these strategies, however, is likely to sustain the church in its mission. More likely, we may learn from and with Jews the sustaining power of imaginative remembering, the ongoing, lively process of traditioning that is sure to be marked by ideological interest that, in the midst of such distinctiveness, may find fresh closures of reality not "conformed to this world." The preaching, teaching, and study of the Torah is in order to "set one's heart" differently, to trust and fear differently, to align oneself with an alternative account of the world.[5] All this Israel fashioned and practiced—at once *imaginatively* resolved, *ideologically* driven, and *inspired* beyond interest—under the large, long, fierce voice of Moses.

III

Thus the traditioning process that pursues a canonical intentionality[6] and that eventuates in a canonical shape is a remarkable achievement whereby a complexity of "bits and pieces" of tradition of many kinds is drawn together in a more or less coherent unity.[7] The "more or less" quality of that unity is to be taken seriously in the interpretation of any particular text, because some texts adhere to canonical coherence more, wherein the original meaning of the tradition readily yields to interpretive imposition. Conversely, some adhere to that "canonical coherence" less, wherein the original meaning of the tradition persists. The traditioning process itself, over a long period and through many efforts, was not able to be singularly consistent about transposition and transformation of appropriated materials. For that reason an attentive reading of the material must allow for "more or less" in varying dimensions. This "more or less" quality of the final form of the text has, on the one hand, produced rather tight and intense church interpretation that accents unity by the "more" of canonical coherence; in response, not surprisingly, such church interpretation has produced an academic response of "less," whereby the complexity and variation of the tradition is more fully accented and appreciated than is the canonical coherence. This endless interpretive tension, often contrasting church interpretation and academic interpretation, is not surprising. It is in the end inescapable, precisely because the tension of "more or less" is readily evident in the final form of the text itself.

As we consider the shape of the Torah in its canonical coherence, we may observe three matters that are roughly consensus in interpretive practice. First, the canonical coherence of the whole of the literature is organized around only a few core theological claims, claims that continue to be central in the interpretive life of the synagogue and the church. These themes have been enunciated by Martin Noth in critical fashion and by Gerhard von Rad in theological exposition.[8] The conventional catalog of such themes includes the following:

Creation	Genesis 1–11
Ancestors	Genesis 12–50
Exodus	Exodus 1–15
Wilderness sojourn	Exodus 16–18
Sinai commands	Exodus 19:1–Numbers 10:10
Wilderness sojourn	Numbers 10:11–36:13
Sinai commands extrapolated	Deuteronomy

These themes gather to themselves a rich variety of already existing materials; for the most part the materials in their complexity serve the theological theme under which they are subsumed.

On this list of themes, two observations are important.

1. It has been noticed, especially by James Sanders, that the Torah ends at the death of Moses in Deuteronomy 34, looking into the land of promise, but still short of entry into the land.[9] Thus the narrative literature serves the condition, circumstance, and hope of the landless, particularly sixth-century exiles at the time of the formation of the literature. Subsequently, many generations of Diaspora Jews have been served by the same motif. That narrative termination, which stops short of fulfillment in the land of promise, has been lined out, moreover, in elegant fashion in Hebrews 11 with its remarkable

---

Midrashic Moment: Deuteronomy 34

Near the end of his last public speech, delivered on April 3, 1968, at a rally to support striking sanitation workers in Memphis, Martin Luther King Jr. refers explicitly to the end of the Torah, where Moses dies outside the promised land, having been allowed by God to see it but not allowed to enter with the people. "He's allowed me to go up to the mountain," says King, "and I've looked over. And I've seen the promised land. I may not get there with you. But I want you to know tonight, that we, as a people, will get to the promised land." In a strategy that means to fight against both hopelessness and complacency, King's speech replicates the open-ended and forward-looking nature of the Torah, which ends with the promised goal in sight but not yet in possession. It is impossible to read or listen to that speech today (numerous recordings of it exist), knowing as we do that King would be assassinated the very next day, without being moved both by King's tragic prescience with regard to his fate and his hopeful commitment to justice through solidarity.

---

conclusion: "Yet all these, though they were commended for their faith, did not receive what was promised, since God had provided something better so that they would not, apart from us, be made perfect" (Heb. 11:39–40).

The tradition itself knows exactly where the narrative story should end and knows why it ends there: because the tradition is open to fulfillment for that which it awaits in hope. This open-ended hope is not "failure,"[10] but a sense of dynamism of reality in the hands of the future-creating God. This hope in such a God, moreover, coheres with the characteristic lived reality of the community of faith, Jews and Christians, that the promises are not fully kept, that hopes are not fully realized, and that history has not come visibly to the full rule of YHWH. Such fullness is well promised and well hoped, but unmistakably not in hand.

2. The Torah in authoritative form articulates the primal themes of faith for nearly all that is to follow, Jewish and Christian. There is, however, one important exception: the later emergence of the Jerusalem establishment, not situated in the text of the Old Testament until the books of Samuel and Kings (see esp. 2 Sam. 5:6–10; Ps. 78:67–72).

This achievement of David and Solomon must be held in abeyance in the telling of the normative story, though one may recognize in the ancestral narratives of Genesis some hints of anticipation of David and Jerusalem, since the makers of the final form of the texts were fully familiar with that subsequent development. In any case, the normative literature is constructed so that Israel still awaits *kingship* that will issue for both Jews and Christians in messianic hope, and *temple* that for Jews and Christians will issue an expectation of YHWH's full and palpable presence in the community. It is clear that both themes of *Messiah* and *presence*, in Christian parlance, serve the theological claims made in the church for Jesus, who is confessed to be the awaited Messiah and the bodied presence of God.

Second, while the traditioning process is complex and long-term, scholars now accept that the final form of the text reflects the work and conviction of two great *theological-interpretive trajectories* working in and around the exilic period, both of which have deep roots in earlier phases of Israel's life and faith. The final form of the text is the editorial achievement of the Priestly and Deuteronomic traditions.

The *Priestly tradition*, with primary attentiveness to holiness and the cultic institutional practices that enhance holiness, produced the final form of Genesis–Numbers. These materials, organized around a system of "generations" in order to ensure genealogical continuity in a community under threat, focused upon cultic arrangements of holiness in the Sinai traditions of Exodus 25–31, 35–40, Leviticus, and Numbers 1–10. These materials of command are prefaced by narratives that concern, for example, the authorization of the Sabbath (Gen. 2:1–4a) and circumcision (Gen. 17).

The *Deuteronomic tradition* that introduced covenant into Israelite interpretive tradition contributes the book of Deuteronomy to the Torah. It is a widely held hypothesis that the "historical narrative" of Joshua, Judges, Samuel, and Kings is informed by Deuteronomy and its interpretive *Tendenz*.[11] Deuteronomy, in contrast to the Priestly tradition, is concerned for the right ordering of the political-economic life of Israel, though it is not without interest in cultic holiness.

These two traditions provide very different interpretive accents and surely arise in different circles of traditionists. It is of enormous importance that the Torah, in its final form, has juxtaposed the two traditions, thereby assuring that the primal canon of ancient Israel is pluralistic, giving prominence to traditions that were in intense contestation with each other. It is, as a consequence, not a surprise that the ongoing interpretive work of Judaism and Christianity continues the vigorous contestation that is already present in the canonical text. That contestation, as a continuing enterprise in text and in interpretation, is crucial to the character of faith, because the contestation rooted in the plurality of traditions assures that the canonical claim of the text can never be safely and finally reduced to a closed, settled package of teaching. The pluriform character of the text assures an endless dynamism in interpretation that inescapably requires that interpretation should be contestation.

Third, it is evident that the plot of the Torah, constituted by the interface of Priestly and Deuteronomic traditions and shaped by the focus upon dominant interpretive themes, moves from God's creation of "heaven and earth" and the ordering of the "earth" ('erets) to the brink of the "promised land" ('erets). Thus the canonical horizon of the Torah that begins in a cosmic focus upon the earth devolved into a focus upon Israel's destiny and future, though never losing sight of the larger vista. The move from 'erets as "earth" to 'erets as "promised land" is accomplished in the ancestral narratives of Genesis 12–36, whereby the ancestors of promise are assured a special land, a land not yet received at the close of the Torah. There is no doubt, in any case, that the promised land "flowing with milk and honey" will manifest all of the blessings of fertility, fruitfulness, and abundance that belong to creation; consequently, the land of Israel is a "good land" as a representative embodiment of creation that God has called "very good" (Gen. 1:31).

The move from *creation* to *land of promise*, however, is wrought in the Torah only by way of Sinai. The Sinai tradition of Exodus 19:1–Numbers 10:10 occupies nearly one-half of the material of the Torah. This corpus of commandments is complex and multilayered; like the narrative, it has been formed through a multifaceted interpretive practice that asserts the terms of land reception that are congruent with the Creator's ordering of all creation.[12] It is evident in ancient and in modern practice that the land as gift and as possession, taken by itself, generates and is generated through self-serving ideology. It is precisely the teaching of the Torah on holiness toward God and fidelity toward neighbor (so powerfully articulated at Sinai) that curbs the propensity, ancient and contemporary, to treat the gift of land as an unconditional entitlement.

Thus the large plot sequence of *creation–Sinai tradition–land* holds together the sense of entitled land so celebrated in ancient Israel and the conditionality of obedience as a precondition of the land. These two matters in some tension—*unconditional entitlement* and the *condition of obedience*—are held together in the gift of YHWH, who is disclosed as one who is generous in gift and sovereign in demand. Over the generations, Israel pondered this restless interface that is rooted in YHWH's own character. The fact that the traditioning process could never escape the tension that is definitional for Israel is, perhaps, the reason that the tradition continued to develop through layers and layers of rearticulation. Sam Balentine has nicely seen how this tradition has served as a concrete resource for communities of faith whose anticipation of the gift of land was a more powerful reality than the possession and settlement of the land itself:

> The process that leads to the canonization of the Pentateuch works intentionally to preserve a vision of another world where the hope and promise of God's creational design remain vital and attainable. In the surety of this vision, the faith community in Yehud [i.e., Judah] survives. Consigned to live at the border—between the realities that manage and extend the status quo and the enduring trust that rests in future possibilities, elusive but real—Yehud finds in the Torah's vision the foundation for building a new and viable self-identity.[13]

The whole in all of its complex, multilayered parts is for the believing communities the Word of God/revelation/guidance for how to hope for and live in the world over which YHWH presides. As Rabbi Ben Bag Bag said of the Torah many centuries ago: "Turn it and turn it, for everything is in it" (Mishnah *'Abot* 5:22).

Questions for Reflection

1. No matter where you are on the Christian theological spectrum, there is much to learn from the imaginative remembering of Judaism and Torah. How do you begin to "set your heart" to align yourself with God's account of the world?

2. The beauty of the text is its pluriform character. Many traditions and beliefs can be contained within the text, which creates an "endless dynamism in interpretation" that can lead to a more robust faith. Do you see the text in this way? Does this perspective lead you to approach the text differently?

3. Though Brueggemann argues that reading the biblical text in both Jewish and Christian contexts is an ongoing interpretive work, some people of faith do not hold that view and instead adopt a closed and reduced idea of the biblical text. Where do you think this leads? What has come of this type of reductionist approach throughout history and in our current context?

4. In Martin Luther King's speech to the sanitation workers on strike in Memphis, he recounts how Moses saw the promised land but realized that he would never enter it, though the people would. King reminds his listeners and readers that they may be able to envision and hope for what is to come, but not yet be in possession, through the open-ended nature of the Torah. Do you feel this in your own journey of faith? In what ways are you able to envision the promised land? What pathways do you see to get there?

Chapter 4

God's Promises and Provision

Exegetical and Homiletical Focus

Exegetical Focus: Hope in the Ancestral Stories

The first eleven chapters of Genesis are among the most important in
Scripture. The prehistory of Genesis 1:1–11:29 focuses on the narratives of creation, garden, Cain and Abel, the flood, and the tower.
Across the different stories, the central concern is with the large
issue of the relation of creator and "creature," which is understood in
diverse ways, sometimes as undifferentiated creation, sometimes as
human and nonhuman creatures in differentiated relation, and sometimes as human creatures alone. In these texts, the theologians of
Israel face the basic mystery of life upon which all social well-being
depends. The texts appropriate materials from the common traditions
of the Near East. But they handle and utilize them in a peculiarly
theological way. The theologians who work in a distinctively Israelite way in Genesis 1–11 want to affirm at the same time (a) that the
ultimate meaning of creation is to be found in the heart and purpose
of the creator (6:5–7; 8:21) and (b) that the world has been positively
valued by God for itself (1:31). It must be valued by the creatures to
whom it has been provisionally entrusted.

This delicate statement is neither mythological (confining meaning to the world of the gods) nor scientific (giving creation its own
intrinsic meaning). The affirmations of Israel are dialectical. They

Editor's note: The following originally appeared in a commentary on the book of Genesis,
which is why it is more singularly focused on the details of the text. These stories revolve
around God's promises and human responses of hope for the fulfillment of those promises.

45

affirm two realities in tension with each other, neither of which is true by itself. We have no adequate word for this dialectical affirmation about creation, which is peculiarly Israelite. It is probably best to use the word "covenantal," as Barth has urged.[1] That word affirms that the creator and the creation have to do with each other decisively. Neither can be understood apart from the other. These perceptions lead to two overriding theological affirmations.

First, the creator has a purpose and a will for creation. The creation exists only because of that will. The creator continues to address the creation, calling it to faithful response and glad obedience to his will. The creation has not been turned loose on its own. It has not been abandoned. Nor has it been given free rein for its own inclinations. But the purposes of the creator are not implemented in a coercive way, nor imposed as a tyrant might. The creator loves and respects the creation. The freedom of creation is taken seriously by the creator. Therefore, his sovereign rule is expressed in terms of faithfulness, patience, and anguish.

Second, the creation, which exists only because of and for the sake of the creator's purpose, has freedom to respond to the creator in various ways. As the texts indicate, the response of creation to creator is a mixture of faithful obedience and recalcitrant self-assertion. Both are present, though the negative response tends to dominate the narrative.

These theological affirmations, then, set the main issues and the dramatic tensions of the text: the faithful, anguished, respectful purpose of the creator and creation's mixed response of obedience and recalcitrance.

We are so familiar with these texts that we have reduced them to cliches. But we should not miss the bold intellectual effort that is offered here, nor the believing passion that informs that intellectual effort. Israel is thinking a new thought. In the use of their faithful imagination, Israel's theologians have articulated a new world in which to live. Their gift to us is an alternative way of discerning reality. It is a way that neither abdicates in "mythology" nor usurps in autonomy. It is a way in which obedience is known to be the mode of the world willed by God. But this is not obedience that is required or demanded. It is a grateful obedience embodied as doxology. These texts ask if this world of mixed response can become a creation of doxology (see Rev. 11:15–19).

I. The Embraced Call of God (Gen. 11:30–25:18)

By faith Abraham obeyed when he was called to go out to a place that he was to receive as an inheritance. . . . By faith Sarah herself received power to conceive, even when she was past the age, since she considered him faithful who had promised. . . .
    By faith Abraham, when he was tested, offered up Isaac, and he who had received the promises was in the act of offering up his only son. . . . He considered that God was able even to raise him from the dead. (Heb. 11:8, 11, 17, 19 ESV)

Beginning in Genesis 11:30, the one who calls the worlds into being now makes a second call. This call is specific. Its object is identifiable in history. The call is addressed to aged Abraham and to barren Sarah. The purpose of the call is to fashion an alternative community in creation gone awry, to embody in human history the power of the blessing. It is the hope of God that in this new family all human history can be brought to the unity and harmony intended by the one who calls.

In its canonical form, Genesis is clear about two things. First, the God who forms the world is the same God who creates Israel. It is the same God who calls creation and who calls the community of faith. This same God works his powerful, creative purpose and intervenes in surprising, redemptive ways. The call to Sarah and Abraham has to do not simply with the forming of Israel but with the re-forming of creation, the transforming of the nations. The stories of this family are not ends in themselves but point to God's larger purposes. Thus Genesis 11:30–25:18 must be read in the context of Genesis 1:1–11:29.

Second, it is clear that Abraham and Sarah, in contrast to the resistant, mistrustful world presented in Genesis 1–11 (with the important exceptions of creation in chapter 1 and Noah), are responsive and receptive. They fully embrace the call of God. It is speculative to ask if this is the only family God has called in this way (see Amos 9:7). But it is unambiguous that this family has responded in a peculiar and faithful way. In this narrative, there is a striking correspondence between God's call and the response of Abraham and Sarah. It is that correlation that offers to us the theme of *promise and faith* around which the narrative revolves. In their present form, regardless of their earlier history, each of the texts must be considered in relation to the issues of promise and faith. *Promise* is God's mode of presence in these narratives. The promise is God's power and will to create a new future sharply discontinuous with the past and the present. The promise is God's resolve to form a new community wrought only by miracle and reliant only on God's faithfulness. *Faith* as response is the capacity to embrace that announced future with such passion that the present can be relinquished for the sake of that future.

II. Critical Issues

The critical issues in the Abraham-Sarah narrative must be acknowledged even though they cannot all be solved.

1. It is clear that the literature of Genesis 11:30–25:18 is the result of a complex development of tradition. The completed narrative is made up of various elements gathered around several distinct themes. Scholars have grouped and analyzed the materials in a variety of ways. They include the following elements:

   a) Materials related to the family of Abraham
      (1) *Sarah* materials
         (a) Sarah as the endangered wife (Gen. 12:10–20; 20)
         (b) Sarah and her two sons (Gen. 16; 18:1–15; 21)
         (c) Sarah's death (Gen. 23)
      (2) *Lot* materials
         (a) Lot and the land (Gen. 13)
         (b) Sodom and Gomorrah (Gen. 19:1–29)
         (c) Lot and his daughters (Gen. 19:30–38)
      (3) *Isaac* materials
         (a) The near-sacrifice (Gen. 22)
         (b) A wife for Isaac (Gen. 24)
      (4) The *Genealogy* of Abraham (25:1–18)
   b) Materials related to God's covenant with Abraham
      (1) The older tradition (Gen. 15:7–21)
      (2) The later tradition (Gen. 17)
   c) A narrative of public events (Gen. 14)
   d) Theological affirmations
      (1) The initial promise (Gen. 12:1–9)
      (2) The faith of Abraham (Gen. 15:1–6)

(3) The new righteousness (Gen. 18:16–32)
(4) The testing of Abraham (Gen. 22)

The materials are not easily contained in any scheme, and this arrangement should not be considered authoritative. What we have is a collection of narratives. It is in the nature of narrative to be distinctive and peculiar. For that reason, no pattern should be suggested which diminishes the particular character of the materials.

2. The common judgment among scholars is that these texts may include very old materials, even though the historical rootage of old materials cannot be recovered. Coupled with these older materials, which do not have great theological intentionality, there are more reflective materials that do make intentional theological affirmations.

As we have them, the texts are a combination of the two kinds of materials. Exposition must attempt to let these two perspectives interact with each other. This means that the early *traditional materials* must be dealt with as they are, with their own power. But at the same time, they must be seen through the lens of the later *theological affirmations* that transform them. As a result, the older materials become vehicles for affirmations they did not originally claim.

Finally, we must try to hear the texts in their present completed form as they have been brought together in the unity of the canon. When all the materials are thus brought together, they become a statement about the overriding promise of God and the way of that promise in the faith and life of this family.

3. Following Westermann, we may identify four theological statements that can usefully provide the focus of exposition.[2]

a. *Genesis 12:1–9.* The basic theme of radical newness is announced. This unit presents the primary summons of God, the ready answer of Abraham, and the derivative blessing to the nations. As Wolff has observed, that blessing may be seen as an organizing principle relating Abraham to a variety of peoples, including Pharaoh (12:10–21), Melchizedek (14:17–24), Ishmael (21:9–21), and Moab and Ammon (19:30–38).[3]

b. *Genesis 15:1–6.* This text provides a singular statement on the meaning of faith (see v. 6). It is this theme that provides a clue to the coherence of the Abraham tradition. The faith of Abraham has become a programmatic element for Paul's exegesis of Abraham in Romans and Galatians and for the subsequent Reformation tradition of justification by grace through faith.

c. *Genesis 18:16–33*. This narrative has not received the attention it merits. The faithfulness of Abraham here is manifested in his bold posture as God's "theological teacher." He urges God to a new notion of righteousness. This text represents one of the most daring theological explorations in the entire narrative.

d. *Genesis 22:1–9*. Concerning the God of Israel, this text boldly affirms the dialectic but crucial unity of God. God is the one who tests (and takes from his people) and the one who provides (and gives what is needed for a future). The placement of this text in the lectionary with the transfiguration narrative of Mark 9:1–9 and with Romans 8:31–39 is suggestive. In the Genesis narrative there is also a transfiguration, the appearance of a "new form of God," quite as radical as the "metamorphosis" of the Markan narrative. It is the unity of *testing/providing* that makes the proximity with Romans 8:31–39 appropriate. It is God's staggering surprise in 22:13 that makes it certain that there is no ultimate separation from him.

III. Theological Affirmations and Possibilities

The long traditioning process behind these materials was not especially concerned about making a coherent theological statement. These materials were a treasured memory that served to construct and maintain the ethos of this people. However, it is reasonable to conclude that over a long period, by means of a shrewd and knowing reshaping, the materials did become a coherent theological statement. They became an earthen vessel for a treasure of faith. It is to that treasure of faith that our exposition addresses itself.

1. In its present form, the governing promise concerns the *land*. The issues are whether God can keep that promise and whether Abraham can live from that promise. But within the frame of the land promise, the promise of *an heir* takes on increasing importance. There can be no fulfillment of the land promise unless there is an heir. The promise of the heir is always in the service of the land promise. In the narrative itself, the promise of an heir receives major attention and gives the narrative its primary dynamic.

These diverse narrations have been shaped into a staggering and suspenseful theological statement. The basic plot moves from profound tension to unexpected resolution. That movement occurs principally between the promise of 12:1–3 and the reiteration of that promise in 22:15 18. The initial struggle is for an heir to receive the land. The heir is finally granted in 21:1–7. Immediately in 22:1–13, the heir is placed in jeopardy. When the heir is risked, the promise is confirmed; afterwards, the suspense is largely gone from the narrative. Genesis 23:1–25:18 is primarily materials of transition that lie outside the main artful presentation. Altogether, the narrative affirms that God will keep his promise and that Abraham and Sarah will trust the promise.

2. The main emphases of the theological affirmation in the transition materials are articulated in the text from Hebrews 11 (cited at the beginning of section I of this chapter). That indicates three dimensions of theological concern.

a. *Hebrews 11:8–10. The promise of a land* is made to a landless people. It does not matter if Abraham is thought to be a nomad, a merchant prince, or a caravanner—all of which are recent scholarly suggestions. In any case, he has no place of his own. The "outlandishness" of the promise should not be missed.

b. *Hebrews 11:11–12. The promise of an heir* is made to a barren, hopeless couple. The first promise of land depends on the fulfillment of the second, on the reality of a second generation. The narrative presses that issue until the birth in Genesis 21. The central text is 18:1–15, in which the promise of a son is shown to be scandalous and impossible. The question of the narrative is the question of all faithful people: "Is anything too wonderful for the LORD?" (v. 14). It is an enduring question for all of biblical faith (cf. Mark 10:23–31).

c. *Hebrews 11:17–19.* Abraham is tested by the *command to offer Isaac.* In the total narrative this might seem a subordinate point. Yet the movement of the promise from Genesis 12:1–3 to Genesis 22:15–18 shows (supported by Heb. 11) that this event is as crucial for the total tradition as are the promises of land and son. It is this event that places everything in jeopardy. The faithfulness of God is called into question. And the responding faithfulness of Abraham is deeply tested. A popular question out of that narrative may be whether God *tests* in such a way. But an even more difficult question is whether

God *provides*. The narrative leads the writer of Hebrews, addressing a community in persecution, to a proclamation of the resurrection. The resurrection is seen as the way in which God incredibly keeps promises against all the data.

The three issues together, (a) believing a land will be given, (b) believing an heir will be born, (c) believing God can provide beyond testing, all press the listening community to the issue of faith.

The tradition affirms Abraham as a "knight of faith" who *does* trust. But the evidence of the individual texts is more mixed than that. To be sure, the moments of faith are profound. He immediately departs to answer the call (Gen. 12:4). He leaves early with his son (22:3). Between the two obedient departures, he trusts the promise (15:6). The trust of Abraham is the main claim of the narrative. It is stated at the beginning (12:3), in the middle (15:6), and at the end (22:1–13).

But Abraham's believing does not occur in a vacuum. He must live in history. So he is not always sure. Thus there is his deception to save his skin (12:10–20; 20:1–18). There is his alternative wife, just in case (16:1–16). There is his clinging to Ishmael, when God has Isaac in mind (17:18). These texts guard against any inclination to interpret Abraham's faith as having been easy or without anguish.

3. The faith to which Abraham is called and for which he is celebrated means the acknowledgment of a particular God. He trusts in a God who can violate religious conventions (18:16–32), shatter normal definitions of reality (18:14), and bring about newness (21:1–7). Isaac—long anticipated, finally given, and then demanded back—is the embodiment of the newness God can bring about in this family of barrenness. There are in the Bible three primary ways of speaking of such radical, unextrapolated newness: (a) creation out of nothing, (b) resurrection of the dead, and (c) justification by grace through faith (Rom. 4:17). In the Abrahamic narrative, it is the birth of Isaac that points to all three.

We have before us a God for whom there is no analogy or parallel. The narrative raises questions about and protests against a world that is fixed on what is safe, predictable, and controllable. This text affirms that there is a discontinuity between what is and what is promised by God. The newness that God has promised will not be wrought from the things that are, but will be given freshly by God in his powerful faithfulness. This faith, as Abraham understands so well in chapter 22, places in question everything that is. God has issued a call and made a promise against the barrenness and land-lessness of this family. He forms a minority community, "the Abra-hamic minority," based on nothing more reliable than the laugh of Sarah (21:6), which anticipates the "Easter laugh" of the community around Jesus.

4. It does not surprise us that the New Testament has found the Abraham narratives especially freighted. They express the "gospel beforehand" (Gal. 3:8). The main themes of the gospel are either stated or anticipated here. This is evident in the reflections of Hebrews 11. It is equally clear in the Pauline treatment of faith in Romans 4 and Galatians 3–4. Of course, the contrast of Isaac and Ishmael and the allegorical pairing of Sarah/Hagar, Zion/Sinai in Galatians 4 are beyond the Genesis narrative itself. But Paul has surely understood the narrative faithfully on the main point of the children of promise born to freedom (Gal. 4:31–5:1).

Special mention may be made of the cryptic and threatening state-ment of John the Baptist in Matthew 3:9:

> Do not presume to say to yourselves, "We have Abraham as our ancestor"; for I tell you, God is able from these stones to raise up children to Abraham.

The news of the gospel and the reality of new life depend only upon the will of God. The statement of John and the entire Abrahamic nar-rative speak a judgment against those who cling to their antipromise ways of identity.

5. The Abrahamic narrative offers rich opportunity for exposition. The narrative sets itself against every worldview and ideology that regards the world as settled and fixed. It is ironic and troubling that the modern world, which so celebrates freedom, also tends to believe that present life is closed and self-contained. It is an assumption of the modern world (in which our exposition must be done) that there will be no genuine newness, no really independent gift yet to be given. Such ideologies press persons either (a) to *inordinate pride* that imagines the world has been completely entrusted to us and that we may construct our own future out of the present, or (b) to *deep despair* that believes the present world of inequity and oppression

is forever and that there is no power in heaven or on earth that can make real change. Both the ideology of pride and the ideology of despair presume that the world is essentially a human artifact, that all possibilities are comprehended in human capacities for good or for ill.

Against such judgments, the Abraham narrative proposes an alternative reality that rescues from both pride and despair. The narrative affirms that the world has not been entrusted to humanity. In inscrutable graciousness, God has retained the amazing gift of life.

The "gospel beforehand" (cf. Gal. 3:8) is good news to those who despair. It announces that what the world has thought impossible is possible by the power of God (cf. Gen. 18:14; Mark 10:27). It is possible by the promise of God to be delivered from the barren world of oppression, injustice, and hopelessness. If the despairing ones listen to these texts, they will be able to join in the "Easter laugh" of Sarah (Gen. 21:6).

The "gospel beforehand" is shattering to those who come to the world in strident pride. This narrative is the assertion that our best laid plans are called into question. It affirms that not all our deceptions (cf. 12:10–20; 20:1–18) or alternative arrangements (16; 17:18) can resist God's odd ordering of things. This narrative calls life into question in ways that are good news and bad news. Some are given new hope by the narrative. Others are shattered by the same narrative but, it is hoped, on the way to newness.

6. Such an understanding of the Abraham and Sarah narratives permits us to discern afresh what Jesus, son of Abraham, is about. For Jesus of Nazareth, "kingdom of God" (Mark 1:14–15) is the cipher for the newness that is given by the promise of God. It is the kingdom that gives new life to the barren ones (Luke 7:22). That is a scandal whenever it is given (v. 23). It is the kingdom that comes as a disruptive newness to give life back to the dead. Predictably, it evokes resistance (see Mark 3:5–6). It is the disruption of the kingdom of this age by healing (Mark 5:17).

The threat and the possibility articulated in the narrative of Abraham and Sarah put a crisis before humanity. It is the crisis of deciding to live either *for the promise*, and so disengaging from the present barren way of things, or to live *against the promise*, holding on grimly to the present ordering of life. Luke's summary about

Jesus is a conclusion we might expect in response to the news of our narrative: (a) Some *resist the promise*: "The chief priests, the scribes, and the leaders of the people kept looking for a way to kill him" (Luke 19:47). (b) Some *welcome the promise*: "All the people were spellbound by what they heard" (Luke 19:48). Faith in God's promise is a possibility that the world sees as scandalous. The world will do what it can to eliminate the promise and to crush the "impossible possibility" with ideologies of conformity, oppression, "the good life," self-realization. The promise jeopardizes everything the world holds dear. But for all of that, Sarah and the community of Abraham have the last laugh (Gen. 21:6; Luke 6:21; John 16:20; Heb. 11:12). It is that laugh that is the ground for this ludicrous storytelling, which is both our deepest threat and our best hope.

Homiletical Focus: "The Future: Trust but Verify"*

In dealing with the Soviet Union, Ronald Reagan skillfully used the phrase "trust, but verify." He was pressed to "trust" by people who were passionate for some restraint on the arms race that was eating us alive. But he did not want to be soft, so he qualified "trust" by requiring inspections, evidence, and verification. That combination worked for him, and maybe for us in our Lenten journey of faith.

I

Paul writes this lyrical chapter, Romans 4, to the church in Rome. He writes to the church as it is deciding how to move forward, not a bad text for a church that is between pastors, that must think about its future. There are hints that some in that church in Rome did not want to think about the future.

Maybe they preferred to think about the present in ways that generated quibbles and quarrels or debates about what was required in

---

Editor's note: What follows is a sermon that focuses on God's promises to the ancestors in Genesis, which Brueggemann delivered during Lent on March 4, 2012. The lectionary texts for the day were Genesis 17:1–7; 15–16; Psalm 22:23–31; Romans 4:16–21; Mark 8:31–38.

order to pass muster about faith and about conduct and about who was best and the most qualified to be in leadership. Maybe they were preoccupied with their celebrated past. The Jewish Christians liked to think about how they had kept all the requirements of Torah; the Gentile members of the church liked to brag about their freedom, which was grounded in the reasonableness of their thinking. They debated past and present, with all their pride and their scruples, and their passion for control, and perhaps they debated about what to give up for Lent in order to be more intentionally people of faith.

II

But Paul abruptly changes the subject on the church in Rome. He tells them that their past—Jewish or Gentile—is not very interesting, because no one is really qualified because of their past, because all have sinned and fallen short. He tells them that the present measuring up to requirements for faith in the present tense should not be absolutized. So do not, he says, linger over a proud past or a reoccupying present tense. Because it is all about the future to which God is summoning us, the future that God is creating before our very eyes. Trust that future and walk into it.

III

Paul reaches back to Father Abraham, the oldest guy in the memory of Israel, as a harbinger of God's future. You remember Abraham from our reading in Genesis. He was ninety-nine years old, and he had no heir and no way to get an heir. Paul says he was "as good as dead," which means he had no chance for a son. This preoccupation with "reproductive possibility" indicates how contemporary the Bible is! Without an heir in that ancient patriarchal world, life was a total dead end. But God comes into his cul-de-sac and announces a future that required incredible trust on Abraham's part. A son would be given!

> You shall be the ancestor of a multitude of nations. . . . I have made you the ancestor of a multitude of nations. I will make you

exceedingly fruitful; and I will make nations of you, and kings shall come from you. I will establish my covenant between me and you, and your offspring after you throughout their generations, for an everlasting covenant, to be God to you and to your offspring after you. And I will give to you, and to your offspring after you, the land where you are now an alien, all the land of Canaan. (Gen. 17:4b–8)

What a mouthful! The one with no future will have a full and rich and glorious future, all because of the gift of God.

Paul takes up this old memory and transposes it into the church's future. Paul, with his uncommon imagination, magnifies this strange gift of an heir with other lyrical claims. He says,

It depends on faith, in order that the promise may rest on grace and be guaranteed to all his descendants, not only to the adherents of the law but also to those who share the faith of Abraham. (Rom. 4:16)

It all rests on grace, the inexplicable gift of God's grace in God's generosity that shatters all of our categories. It requires only faith, only trust, only readiness to receive.

If that is not impressive enough, try these two extrapolations that Paul offers:

[W]ho gives life to the dead. (v. 17)

It's all about God's capacity to create new life and new possibility beyond all of our control and explanation. It turns on the resurrection of Jesus, just as Jesus promised his disciples in our Gospel reading.

It is this newness that is sung in our psalm. The psalm we read begins, "My God, my God, why have you forsaken me?" But the psalm ends in wild praise and thanks, because God has raised this desolate psalmist to new life. In the same way the church lives in the wake of Easter, celebrating that God overcomes the power of death and refuses to let Jesus be negated by the power of the empire. Talk about a future!

But Paul goes further with this chill-bump-producing affirmation:

[W]ho . . . calls into existence the things that do not exist. (v. 17)

This is a summoning of creation out of nothing, this God who has said, "Let there be light," "Let there be life," "Let there be dry land," "Let there be new possibility." Talk about a future!

The lyric of Paul is outrageous in its extravagance; but it is the ground of faith. Paul links these three claims for God's future:

- a baby born to this aged couple
- a dead man raised to Easter life
- a world made out of nothing

A family, a life, a world! All things new by the good generous work of God who refuses to let us remain in a failed past or in a mesmerizing present.

The church lives by the surprises of God, and we situate our modest daily newnesses in that big lyric . . . a life changed, a sinner forgiven, a meal served, a garden planted, a mission undertaken, a friendship that transforms, and before we know it, we say, after the Gospel and with great exuberance:

The blind see.
The deaf hear.
Lepers are cleansed.
The lame walk.
The dead are raised.
The poor rejoice,
because this is the gift of God in which we trust.

IV

All that is required is trust. All that is needed is to give ourselves over to the strange, inexplicable power for life that breaks all the old resistances of fear, anger, anxiety, and despair. So it is with our father, Abraham. He trusted. His trust was taken by God as full obedience. Such trust is not such an easy matter. We hold ourselves back. We calculate. We wait to see. We are suspicious. But that is the plunge of love when we risk ourselves into the power of bottomless love. That is what we do when we fall in love. Abraham, in that instant of promise, fell in love with God. And so he reached into the future given by God. Genesis says only that "he went."

But Paul says more:

- verse 20: No distrust made him waver concerning the promise of God;
- verse 20: He grew strong in his faith;
- verse 21: He was fully convinced that God was able to do what he had promised.

The long history of faith, with all the saints, is the story of walking into the future given by God. Lent is a time for sorting this out. Popular Lent is too much preoccupied with guilt and repentance. But not here. Lent is rather seeing how to take steps into God's future so that we are no longer defined by what is past and no longer distracted by what we have treasured or feared about the present. Lent is for embracing:

- the baby given to old people
- resurrection to new life in Easter
- the offer of a new world made by God from nothing

And so in this great church, a new future of gospel possibility.

V

But I have not yet come to "verify." Not just trust: verify . . . seek evidence . . . require facts. Faith around evidence that comes in narrative form:

Abraham's faith came to verification with Isaac:

By faith he received power of procreation, even though he was too old—and Sarah herself was barren—because he considered him faithful who had promised. Therefore from one person, and this one as good as dead, descendants were born, "as many as the stars of heaven and as the innumerable grains of sand by the seashore." (Heb. 11:11–12)

The faith of the church is received by testimony. So Paul writes

that he appeared to Cephas, then to the twelve. Then he appeared to more than five hundred brothers and sisters at one time, most of whom are still alive, though some have died. Then he appeared to James, then to all the apostles. Last of all, as to one untimely born, he appeared also to me. (1 Cor. 15:5–8)

If you want verification that God's promises are kept, you will not find that verification among the new atheists who have reduced everything to a tight little package of reasonableness that easily explains everything away. Nor will we find verification among the fundamentalists who have God in such a box that there can be no room for inexplicable gifts. You will find verification among the daily performances of the trusting ones who live out their trust in ways that the world terms foolish:

- The verification is in a church ready to be venturesome into God's future.
- The verification is in a church that pays attention to those dis-qualified by the capitalist system.
- The verification is in the acceptance of those who are unacceptable.
- The verification is in the commitment of time to neighbors when we prefer to have that time for ourselves.
- The verification is in the telling of hard truth about the world, and that in a culture of denial.
- The verification is in the slant toward justice and peacemaking in a world that loves violence and exploitation too much.
- The verification is in footing the bill for neighborliness and mercy when we have many other bills to pay.
- The verification is in lives that give testimony before the authori-ties who want to silence and intimidate and render irrelevant.

It turns out that the world teems with verification, concerning babies from the barren ones, lives that have surged in the midst of death, hurts that have been healed, estrangements that have been rec-onciled, enslavements that have turned to freedom, all around us, particular, concrete, specific, for people like us.

Ronald Reagan's move insisting on "trust and verify" was in fact a complex, complicated, partial accomplishment, much less clear than his simple rhetoric might have suggested. So the church's invitation to "trust and verify" is also complex, complicated, and partial. But it is decisive for us. So imagine, in this Lenten season, moving beyond treasured pasts, moving beyond precious present-tense arrangements to new God-given prospects. It is no wonder that the psalmist can at the end sing:

> From you comes my praise in the great congregation;
>   my vows I will pay before those who fear him.
> The poor shall eat and be satisfied;
>   those who seek him shall praise the LORD.
> May your hearts live forever!
> All the ends of the earth shall remember
>   and turn to the LORD;
> and all the families of the nations
>   shall worship before him.
> For dominion belongs to the LORD,
>   and he rules over the nations.
>   Ps. 22:25–28

It is our song too. We are on our way rejoicing . . . into God's future.

Questions for Reflection

1. The relationship between creator and creation is set up as a tension between the faithful purposes of the creator and how creation responds in obedience. As you experience creation, as well as being part of creation, how are you responding to the creator? In what ways are you taking care of creation and being obedient to the creator?

2. In Brueggemann's breakdown of Genesis, he states that God is the one who tests and the one who provides, and that the unity of testing/providing is crucial. What do you think about this statement? How have you experienced the testing/providing unity of God in your own life or in your community?

3. Believing does not occur in a vacuum. We live within the contexts of our own realities and experiences. Trusting in a God who goes against the norm of those realities and brings newness may be hard, because there is always something radical entailed. Have you felt this unease before as you follow the creative God? Where did that come from? How were you able to sustain faithful obedience?

4. The narrative of the "gospel beforehand" is both good news to the ones who live in deep despair and shattering to the ones who are steeped in inordinate pride or privilege. Where are you on this spectrum right now? Do you find yourself looking at the world from a place of being neglected and abandoned, and being completely overwhelmed? Do you find yourself in a very privileged place, certain that your plans are secure? Or somewhere in between? How does hope speak to you, where you are?

PART THREE

The Prophets:
Hope for Restoration

Chapter 5

The Prophets

Deep Memories, Passionate Convictions, and New Hopes

*T*here is no doubt that the Torah (Pentateuch) constitutes the primary, normative Scripture of Judaism. In the complete canonical tradition of the Hebrew Bible, it is conventional to divide the non-Torah parts of the text into two units, the Prophets and the Writings. The prophetic canon comprises eight books: the four books that constitute the Former Prophets: Joshua, Judges, Samuel, and Kings (note that Ruth is not included in this sequence in the Hebrew Bible); and the four books that constitute the Latter Prophets: Isaiah, Jeremiah, Ezekiel, and the Twelve (note that Lamentations and Daniel are not included in this sequence in the Hebrew Bible). From a canonical perspective, the Former and Latter Prophets are understood as second to and reliant on the Torah. One might say that the Torah is the articulation—in narrative and in commandment—of the norms of faith and obedience commensurate with the rule of YHWH.

The prophetic canon is a literature that articulates Israel's faith and practice in the rough-and-tumble of historical reality. It is an exercise in rereading the history of Israel and the history of the world according to the gifts and requirements of the God of the Torah. The simple sequence of "Torah, Prophets" is a given of the canon, though the critical situation of the literature is much more complex. There is a likelihood that the Former Prophets draws its theological perspective from Deuteronomy and is thus shaped by Torah literature. In the Latter Prophets, however, the critical reality is very different. It is commonly thought by scholars that the prophetic oracles of the eighth and seventh centuries antedate the final form of the Torah, thus suggesting that the earliest articulation of what became

65

the canonical faith of the Torah may have been first accomplished by the prophets.

In any case, it is clear that the literature of the prophetic canon, in very different circumstances and in very different modes, seeks to do in parallel fashion what the Torah seeks to do, namely, to imagine, articulate, and evoke a world ordered by and responsive to YHWH, the Creator of heaven and earth and the Lord of Israel's covenant.

I. The Former Prophets

The four books of the Former Prophets constitute a sustained narrative account of Israel from the entry into the land of promise until the deportation from Jerusalem out of the land into exile. While popular Christian understanding treats these books as "history," their categorization as "prophetic" in the Jewish canon more adequately captures the final form of their character and horizon. To be sure, this material contains specific references about named (and unnamed) prophets, but the canonical label "Prophets" refers to the material itself and not to specific prophetic personalities. What is prophetic is the capacity to reconstrue all of lived reality—including the history of Israel and the power relations of the known world of the ancient Near East—according to the equally palpable reality (in this reading) of the rule of YHWH.

On the one hand, the material in the Former Prophets is *theological testimony*, that is, a believing effort to give an account of faith, an account of God, albeit a God who is said to be engaged in the lived processes of history. To recognize the material as testimony causes us to have expectations very different from those we might have for the genre of "history." On the other hand, it is clear that the literature, especially in the books of Kings, intends to be *interpretive commentary* on historical reportage that is said to be elsewhere available to the reader. Thus the tradition has what amounts to footnotes that refer readers to other materials if they have an interest in history. (See 1 Kgs. 11:41; 14:19, 29.) That the text is candid in such citation of other materials eases any modern requirement to make the material "history," and lets us receive it for what it is—a theological advocacy for the meaning of reported history when that history is linked to and reconstrued according to the God of the Torah. It is clear that the imposition of the category of "history" on this material is a failure to recognize what is offered or what is intended in the traditioning process.

Moreover, there can be no doubt that according to canonical formation the four books of the Former Prophets constitute a corpus for the faith community that is quite distinct from the five books of the Torah. However, in current scholarship there is an important impulse to treat the nine books of the Torah and Former Prophets together as one extended, coherent narrative that stretches from creation to exile.[1] The hypothesis of such a coherent narrative must disregard the longstanding canonical distinction between Torah and Prophets in order to appreciate the narrative continuity of the whole, a continuity that has the creation of the earth (*'erets*) culminate in loss of land (*'erets*). This impulse to read the whole as a continuous narrative, termed the Primary Narrative, eschews older historical-critical distinctions and particularly eschews the fragmentation that has become the hallmark of source analysis.

If we can for now consider the claim of such a hypothesis, it is nonetheless important to notice the distinction between the first five books and the last four books of what is termed the Primary Narrative, a distinction important not only because of canonical markers, but because of the decisive turn of plot between the two units of material. We may say that the Torah concerns a promise of and eventual entry into the land of promise, a coherent statement that Gerhard von Rad has characterized as a movement from promise to fulfillment.[2] This movement toward and into the land of promise culminates with the crossing of the Jordan. Thus Israel, according to this narrative, arrives at the Jordan River at the beginning of Deuteronomy (see Num. 33:48; Deut. 1:5), pauses at the Jordan for the long interpretive instruction of Moses in the book of Deuteronomy, and then crosses the Jordan in Joshua 3:14–17, an act replicating the exodus:

> [Joshua said] to the Israelites, "When your children ask their parents in time to come, 'What do these stones mean?' then you shall let your children know, 'Israel crossed over the Jordan here on dry ground.' For the LORD your God dried up the waters of the Jordan for you until you crossed over, as the LORD your God did to the

Red Sea, which he dried up for us until we crossed over, so that all the peoples of the earth may know that the hand of the LORD is mighty, and so that you may fear the LORD your God forever." (Josh. 4:21–24)

Thus the Jordan River functions not only as a geographical marker, but as a literary-canonical-theological marker as well.

The Former Prophets tell the narrative of land loss once the Jordan River has been crossed. In bold strokes this narrative details the sustained and recurring disobedience of Israel that culminates in the loss of the land, a disobedience elsewhere sketched in Psalm 106. Thus these four books rooted in Deuteronomy constitute a tale of *land loss* that is commensurate with the Torah narrative of *land gift*. The dual themes of land gift and land loss constitute a single primary narrative, but the Jordan River marks two quite distinct themes within that larger narrative. The land is given, so it is affirmed, according to YHWH's generous fidelity. The land given, however, is not Israel's unconditional possession; rather, it is held in trust according to the stipulations of the Giver, conditions of the land grant that Israel has failed to meet. The outcome is that the community summoned to venture to a new land in Genesis 12:1 is at the end yet again landless and yet again reliant on the old promises that keep open the chance for a new land entry, a reentry that is anticipated in the Latter Prophets.

II. The Latter Prophets

The term "Latter Prophets" refers to four books, those of the prophets Isaiah, Jeremiah, Ezekiel, and the Twelve (Minor Prophets). In the last case, it is generally understood that these twelve small prophetic books constitute a single scroll and thus a fourth prophetic scroll, so that the four Latter Prophets form a symmetrical complement to the Former Prophets, the two groups together constituting the prophetic canon of eight books. It is with these books that we get to what most people think of as prophecy per se, with public orators issuing passionate critique of the religious and political status quo, or speaking truth to power. As we have seen, an understanding of the Former

Midrashic Moment: Elijah and the Messianic Age

The vivid story in 2 Kings 2 of Elijah being taken up alive into heaven as he is walking along with his protégé Elisha ("a chariot of fire and horses of fire separated the two of them, and Elijah ascended in a whirlwind into heaven," v. 11) becomes the basis of an expectation, in both Jewish and Christian thinking, that he is waiting to return from heaven to help usher in the messianic age. So Malachi 4:5 has God promise that "I will send you the prophet Elijah before the great and terrible day of the LORD comes." The deuterocanonical book of Sirach proclaims that "at the appointed time" Elijah will "restore the tribes of Jacob" (Sir. 48:10). The Gospel writers reflect a similar idea (Matt. 16:13–14; Mark 6:14–15; Luke 9:7–8), to the extent that John the Baptist is intentionally portrayed as an Elijah-like figure. To this day, many Jewish Passover meals will include a place setting for Elijah at the table, symbolically representing a hope that he will show up and bring the coming kingdom of God with him.

Prophets entails a recognition that this material is not "history" in the sense that we regularly use that term.

In somewhat parallel fashion, an understanding of the Latter Prophets (Isaiah, Jeremiah, Ezekiel, and the Twelve) entails a refocus away from a popular notion of prophetic *personalities* to prophetic *books*.[3] The prophetic books may have begun in collections of oracles from remembered personalities. In the editorial process, however, the importance and domination of the prophetic personalities recedes almost totally, so that the prophetic books are now the outcome of long-developed traditions that may be seeded by a named personality. In completed form, however, they are the product of an interpretive process that intends to extend the trajectory of faith well beyond the initiating personality.

The several prophetic books reflect very different theological trajectories. For example, the book of Isaiah in final form is a meditation upon the *temple-monarchy* tradition of Jerusalem. The book of Jeremiah, influenced by the same circles that produced the Former Prophets, is oriented to the centrality of *torah*. The book of Ezekiel, preoccupied with *holiness*, has most affinities with the Priestly tradition of the Torah. Thus it is fair to suggest that the three great prophetic books constitute developing interpretive materials that are committed to and reflect different theological passions in Israel, respectively, royal temple, Torah, and holiness traditions. The three together constitute a compendium of major options in Israel's faith.

Special notice may be taken of the fourth scroll among the Latter Prophets, the Book of the Twelve or, as they are called within the church, the Minor Prophets. In critical understanding, each of these twelve prophets is treated as a distinct entity reflecting a distinct personality, even though they are readily grouped, according to critical judgment, chronologically. Thus Hosea, Amos, and Micah are situated in the eighth century BCE; Nahum, Habakkuk, and Zephaniah in the seventh; Haggai, Zechariah, and Malachi in the Persian period. This leaves Joel, Jonah, and Obadiah, books that are, in critical perspective, understood as later books that are canonically situated in a way that no longer reflects a historical placement.

In more recent scholarship, an effort has been made to understand the Book of the Twelve as a coherent scroll with intentional canonical shape. In particular, James Nogalski and Paul House have made forays into this suggestion, which has the practical effect of loosening each prophetic book from a supposed historical context and instead linking each to the literary-canonical context of the extended scroll.[4] This way of thinking seeks to pay attention to the final form of the text, in this case the final form of the Scroll of the Twelve.

These four scrolls, rooted in different personalities and in the service of different interpretive interests and commitments, proceed in a variety of different ways. Having noted these differences, it is nonetheless important also to notice that a certain pattern of interpretation is visible in the several scrolls as each makes the move beyond land loss. Because the Book of the Twelve constitutes a particular problem, I shall comment first upon the three great scrolls of Isaiah, Jeremiah, and Ezekiel, which, for all their variation, are shaped in close parallel around the themes of judgment and restoration:

a. The book of Isaiah is clearly edited so that chapters 1–39 and chapters 40–66 concern, as Brevard Childs has suggested, "old things" under judgment and "new things" of restoration.[5]

b. The book of Jeremiah is more raggedly edited. It is clear that chapters 1–20 are about "pluck[ing] up and . . . pull[ing] down" (Jer. 1:10).

Midrashic Moment: Ezekiel and Poetic Tradition

Ezekiel is famous for his extravagant visions, and as a result becomes a sort of patron saint for visionary poets, including John Milton and William Blake (who claimed to have dined with Ezekiel and Isaiah). In the opening stanzas of T. S. Eliot's long poem *The Wasteland*, the speaker alludes to Ezekiel's call narrative, when God commands the cowering prophet, "O mortal, stand up on your feet, and I will speak with you" (Ezek. 2:1): "What are the roots that clutch, what branches grow / Out of this stony rubbish? Son of man, / You cannot say, or guess, for you know only / A heap of broken images." *The Wasteland* is often thought to be the quintessential *modern* poem, representing a radical break with tradition, which makes it even more striking for the poet to draw on Ezekiel. But if the past is envisioned in *The Wasteland* as rubble, either real or symbolic, Ezekiel is a natural choice for a poetic predecessor, living as he did through the destruction of Jerusalem and of the temple and presenting a clear-eyed vision of it, while nevertheless holding out hope for a future restoration.

The "building and planting" of the Jeremiah tradition is not very clear or well-ordered literarily. We can, nonetheless, observe that the Book of Comfort (Jer. 30–31) plus the narrative of chapter 32 and the collection of promises in chapter 33 constitute a tradition whereby Israel may have "a future with hope" (29:11). In addition to that cluster, we may notice the postcrisis affirmation of (a) a promise to the Baruch remnant (chap. 45); (b) an anticipated demise of oppressive powers (chaps. 46–51), especially the "sinking" of Babylon (chaps. 50–51); and (c) the continuing significance of the exiled Davidic king (52:31–34). Thus, in its own way, the book of Jeremiah reiterates the two themes of judgment and hope in broad parallel to the structure of the book of Isaiah.

c. The book of Ezekiel is symmetrically ordered, so that chapters 1–24 and chapters 25–48, respectively, articulate judgment and hope around the priestly accents of absence and restored divine presence.

All three scrolls together pivot around the loss of city and temple in 587 BCE; all three, each in a distinctive dialect, move decisively beyond loss to focus on the future that YHWH will give. It is worth noting, then, that while the warnings and condemnations concerning the failure of the urban system of Jerusalem are harsh, uncompromising, and unrelenting in these three traditions, the completed form of the text is not focused on judgment. Rather, the articulation of judgment, in each case no doubt rooted in words of the historical person of the prophet, becomes the launching venue for focus on the future to be given in YHWH's promises through YHWH's fidelity. Thus the old stereotype of "prophetic" as connoting righteous indignation and rage is at best a partial truth and likely a caricature, because the prophetic books finally concern the future.

If it is correct that all three prophetic traditions focus on the same themes of judgment and move determinedly toward hope, we may consider why canonical formation included three articulations of the same claim. We may find a clue to this canonical reality by asking again about the relationship of the Prophets to the Torah. To be sure, source analysis in the Torah traditions is now most problematic. While leaving many things undecided in the current state of the question of source analysis, it is nonetheless clear that the two definitive sources of the Torah are the Priestly tradition that gives shape to the Tetrateuch (Genesis–Numbers) and Deuteronomy, which provided the themes for the Former Prophets (Deuteronomic History). Alongside a recognition of the Priestly and Deuteronomic sources, it seems clear that there is a third, perhaps early, source that may still be identified as the Yahwist (J), that is, the source that uses the name of YHWH from the outset of the beginning in Genesis.

These three sources, it is now clear, are not to be understood in terms of unilinear religious development in Israel. Rather they are coexisting advocacies for certain interpretive perspectives in ancient Israel. On the assumption that the interpretive advocacies in the Torah are closely linked to interpretive advocacies in the Prophets, I may suggest that the three great traditions of Isaiah, Jeremiah, and Ezekiel correlate with and are informed by the interpretive advocacies in the Torah:

> It is evident that *Ezekiel* is clearly linked to the *Priestly* traditions of the Torah.
> It is equally evident that *Jeremiah* is closely linked to the traditions of *Deuteronomy*.

It is not so obvious that *Isaiah* is closely related to the *Yahwist tradition*. But it may at least be suggested that the Abrahamic memories that are central to J yield the Davidic and Zion foci so crucial for the Isaiah tradition.

Thus it is possible to see that these prophetic traditions move through judgment and into hope precisely in connection to the Torah sources, whether the sources fund the prophetic tradition or vice versa. Either way, the connections between the two provide an important and suggestive heuristic entry point for interpretation. The relationship between Torah and Prophets is a very old question in Old Testament studies.[6] It is important to recognize in critical study that the two units of canonical material do not flow in a simple sequence, but may be related in quite interactive ways. Thus the interpretive advocacies in the several sources of the Torah show up in these three prophets as interpretive advocacies about the ways to understand divine judgment upon Israel in Jerusalem and, more important, the ways to imagine futures that will yet be given by YHWH. The prophetic canon more explicitly meditates upon the abyss of exile than does the canon of the Torah; the same issues, however, pertain to the Torah traditions as well. Both Torah and Prophets reflect passionately upon the reality of loss and the promise of futures that pertain through and beyond the loss.

d. The Book of the Twelve (Minor Prophets) constitutes a particular concern in canonical consideration, and so merits a particular comment. An older historical-critical approach to the Twelve continues to be important. On that basis, as indicated above, one can with some confidence assign three prophets to the eighth century (Hosea, Amos, Micah), three prophets to the late seventh century (Nahum, Habakkuk, Zephaniah), and three prophets to the early Persian period (Haggai, Zechariah, Malachi). The dating of Obadiah is secure in the Persian period, and that leaves Joel and Jonah somewhat ill defined. The historical placement of the prophets in these several historical locations gives the sequence of the Twelve a rough chronological ordering. More than that, it also hints of early entries that provide *warning and judgment* and late entries on *hope and restoration*. Thus the sequence that is roughly chronological also provides a theological pattern of judgment and hope.

It is clear in present scholarship that such historical-critical under-standings are important but not adequate in themselves for reading this material. Thus the newer scholarship seeks to move beyond his-torical criticism to ask about the corpus of the Twelve and the par-ticular way in which these originally distinctive literary units have been combined. On the one hand, scholars have noticed that within most of the books there is a developing tradition that moves beyond the historical person of the prophet in order to be related to later contexts and crises. On the other hand, scholars are now inclined to consider the Twelve as one canonical statement. Such explora-tions are only at the beginning, and more work remains to be done. It is already apparent, in any case, that the several elements of the Twelve have developed according to familiar themes of judgment and restoration, so that the eighth-century prophets focus more on judgment and the prophets of the Persian period focus much more on hope. Because hope is "the conviction of things not seen" (Heb. 11:1), it is not surprising that hope moves in an apocalyptic direc-tion, that is, toward expectations that move beyond known histori-cal categories.

In completed form it is possible, as with Isaiah, Jeremiah, and Ezekiel, to see that the Twelve is constituted as a meditation about the crisis into the abyss of 587 (or earlier in 721 BCE in northern Israel) and expectations of newness from YHWH beyond the abyss. Thus the traditioning process has taken these diverse materials and shaped them into some theological coherence. It is to be recognized at the same time, however, that the several subunits do not readily or completely yield themselves to a new, larger theological scheme.

As we have seen elsewhere, the traditioning process is only par-tially successful. As a result, the development of the tradition appears to be a tensive, ongoing negotiation between the already extant mate-rials and the interpretive vision that is more or less imposed and that eventuated in the canonical shape of the literature. The success of the canonical enterprise should not be overstated, but must surely be rec-ognized, so that historical-critical understandings are seen to be only partially adequate for the material. The outcome of the traditioning is a literary entity that is a mixed lot holding together in ragged fashion *initial utterances* that have their own say and an *interpretive coher-ence* that both respects and overrides such initial say.

In the lived reality of Israel, the two moves of entry *into the abyss of exile* and movement *beyond the abyss of exile* are defining. One must recognize the exile as the indispensable matrix for Israel's self-understanding, so that the historical reality of exile becomes paradigmatically definitional for Israel.[7] That adherence to historical facts on the ground, however, is further decisively defined by the claim that it is YHWH who presides over both the scattering and the gathering (as in Zech. 10:9–10). While the facts on the ground about history are held to be decisive, the inscrutable reality of YHWH is ultimately the singular agent of both scattering and gathering. Thus the Twelve, as elsewhere in the prophetic literature, is an effort to imagine the vagaries of history with reference to the reality of YHWH. Rolf Rendtorff has suggested one motif that pervades the Twelve that makes YHWH the defining character, namely, the "day of the LORD," the time of YHWH's vigorous assertion of sovereignty.[8] That day is a day of *disaster and scattering*:

> The great day of the LORD is near,
>   near and hastening fast;
> the sound of the day of the LORD is bitter,
>   the warrior cries aloud there.
> That day will be a day of wrath,
>   a day of distress and anguish,
> a day of ruin and devastation,
>   a day of darkness and gloom,
> a day of clouds and thick darkness,
>   a day of trumpet blast and battle cry
> against the fortified cities
>   and against the lofty battlements.
>   Zeph. 1:14–16

But "the day" also becomes a *time of gathering*:

> And the LORD will become king over all the earth; on that day the LORD will be one and his name one.
>   The whole land shall be turned into a plain from Geba to Rimmon south of Jerusalem. But Jerusalem shall remain aloft on its site from the Gate of Benjamin to the place of the former gate, to the Corner Gate, and from the Tower of Hananel to the king's wine presses. And it shall be inhabited, for never again

shall it be doomed to destruction; Jerusalem shall abide in security. (Zech. 14:9–11)

Thus the reiteration of "the day" in this literature brings the whole of Israel's lived experience under the aegis of YHWH's governance. In the end YHWH "will be one and his name one" (Zech. 14:9). The enhancement of YHWH is accomplished, in the large vista of the Twelve, by the restoration of Jerusalem. Jerusalem has no future apart from YHWH, but YHWH has no way of enhancement apart from the well-being of the city and the people for whom YHWH is jealous. Clear to the end of the Twelve, the pervasive themes of repentance, obedience, and hope persist. It cannot be otherwise, because the world is imagined with reference to YHWH, and YHWH's characteristic markings persist through all of the losses in the life of Israel into all of the futures that YHWH will yet give. These themes are the very themes that arise in the Moses tradition and that are entrusted to Joshua at the beginning of the prophetic corpus:

> Only be strong and very courageous, being careful to act in accordance with all the law that my servant Moses commanded you; do not turn from it to the right hand or to the left, so that you may be successful wherever you go. This book of the law shall not depart out of your mouth; you shall meditate on it day and night, so that you may be careful to act in accordance with all that is written in it. For then you shall make your way prosperous, and then you shall be successful. I hereby command you: Be strong and courageous; do not be frightened or dismayed, for the LORD your God is with you wherever you go. (Josh. 1:7–9)

This imaginative insistence on history under the rule of YHWH persists until the last urging of Malachi to Torah obedience (Mal. 4:4) and Malachi's last promise for future well-being (4:5–6).

Thus it is evident that the Latter Prophets have been more or less programmatically shaped and edited into a twofold assertion of God's *judgment* that brings Israel to exile and death, and God's *promise* that brings Israel to a future that it cannot envision or sense for itself. That pattern has been most clearly seen by Ronald Clements:

> It is rather precisely the element of connectedness between the prophets, and the conviction that they were all referring to a single

theme of Israel's destruction and renewal, which has facilitated the ascription to each of them of the message of hope which some of their number had proclaimed after 587 B.C. . . .

In such fashion we can at least come to understand the value and meaning of the way in which distinctive patterns have been imposed upon the prophetic collections of the canon so that warnings of doom and disaster are always followed by promises of hope and restoration.[9]

In his summation, Clements makes a claim that the theme of "death and rebirth" pertains to the entire prophetic canon, Former and Latter, as the canonical material is shaped in response to the defining lived experiences of the interpretive community:

Rather we must see that prophecy is a collection of collections, and that ultimately the final result in the prophetic corpus of the canon formed a recognizable unity not entirely dissimilar from that of the Pentateuch. As this was made up from various sources and collections, so also the Former and Latter Prophets, comprising the various preserved prophecies of a whole series of inspired individuals, acquired an overarching thematic unity. This centered on the death and rebirth of Israel, interpreted theologically as acts of divine judgment and salvation.[10]

We are able to see in the Latter Prophets, as in the Former Prophets, that the canonical material has been transposed with great interpretive intentionality. In the Former Prophets, "history" has been transposed into a massive *theological commentary* on Israel's past. In the Latter Prophets what began as personal proclamation has been transposed into a *theological conviction* around YHWH's promise for the future. Both theological commentary (in the Former Prophets) and theological conviction (in the Latter Prophets) became a normative, but at the same time quite practical, resource for a community living in and through the deep fissure of deportation and displacement. The prophetic canon functions as a resource to protect the community of faith from surrendering to the vagaries of historical circumstance. Seen in this way, the prophetic canon that testifies to YHWH's governance of past, present, and future is an offer of a counterworld, counter to denial and despair, counterrooted in YHWH's steadfast purpose for a new Jerusalem, new torah, new covenant, new temple—all things new:

> Thus says the LORD,
>   who makes a way in the sea,
>   a path in the mighty waters,
> who brings out chariot and horse,
>   army and warrior;
> they lie down, they cannot rise,
>   they are extinguished, quenched like a wick:
> Do not remember the former things,
>   or consider the things of old.
> I am about to do a new thing;
>   now it springs forth, do you not perceive it?
> I will make a way in the wilderness
>   and rivers in the desert.
> The wild animals will honor me,
>   the jackals and the ostriches;
> for I give water in the wilderness,
>   rivers in the desert,
> to give drink to my chosen people,
>   the people whom I formed for myself
> so that they might declare my praise.
>
> Isa. 43:16–21

Questions for Reflection

1. Brueggemann explains that the Former Prophets contain within them theological testimony that gives an account of faith and God in the midst of lived histories. Take time to follow in the footsteps of the Former Prophets and briefly write your own theological testimony within your present context and history. How has God been engaged in your lived history?

2. In the Former Prophets the land that God gives Israel in generous fidelity is not an unconditional possession and is ultimately lost because Israel fails to live faithfully. How does this orient you in your own relationship with earth, the land, and giftedness?

3. The Latter Prophets constitute a rich variety of theological concepts. One major theme within the Latter Prophets is moving from crisis

to newness beyond the crisis. Reflect on Zephaniah 1:14–16, Zechariah 14:9–11, and Isaiah 43:16–21, and ask yourself: How does this relate to me? What is a crisis in my own life, and how has that crisis unfolded into newness?

4. God's judgment, as described by the Latter Prophets, is often hard to process for readers, and yet is always present alongside God's promises. What comes to mind for you when you think about God's judgment? What does it mean to you to think about God's promises and God's judgment as inseparable?

Chapter 6

Hope for Well-Being in Second and Third Isaiah

Exegetical and Homiletical Focus

Exegetical Focus: The Visionary Poetry of Isaiah

For you shall go out in joy,
    and be led back in peace;
the mountains and the hills before you
    shall burst into song,
    and all the trees of the field shall clap their hands.

Isa. 55:12

The book of Isaiah is the beginning of the Latter Prophets. Consequently it stands, in the Hebrew ordering of the books, back to back with Kings, the last book of the Former Prophets. That interface, not visible in the conventional ordering of books in the Christian Bible, is fortuitous, because the books of Kings and Isaiah are together preoccupied with the destiny of Jerusalem. The books of Kings end with an account of the destruction of Jerusalem at the hands of the Babylonians and the ensuing deportation and exile. The book of Isaiah, in its turn, is a meditation, albeit in complex configuration, about the destiny of Jerusalem *into* the crises of exile and the hopeful promise of Jerusalem *out of* exile into new well-being. The book is also the first book of extended poetry in the Old Testament. Although earlier books had poems inset here and there into the narrative, Isaiah gives us chapter upon chapter of high poetic art.

The book of Isaiah, according to most scholars, is rooted in the actual prophetic personality of Isaiah, son of Amoz, whose conventional dates for life in Jerusalem are perhaps 742 to 689 BCE (Isa. 1:1). However, the book of Isaiah, while rooted in the person of Isaiah, has emerged only through a long, extensive, and complex traditioning process, perhaps through a continuous succession of disciples of Isaiah who continue to articulate the general interpretative trajectory of the person of Isaiah (see 8:1), but who were themselves powerful interpreters capable of generating new articulations. More specifically, critical scholarship for over a century has held to the view that the book of Isaiah is constituted into three quite distinct parts that reflect different historical circumstances, different modes of literary articulation, and consequently different theological vistas. To some extent the literature of the book of Isaiah is simply a continued meditation upon the destiny of Jerusalem, a meditation that occurred in separated, random acts of responsiveness to new issues of faith in new circumstances; at the same time, however, it is clear that the final form of the text has some rough intentionality that gives the whole of the book a suggestive coherence.

In the critical consensus, it has long been held that the literature pertaining to *Isaiah of the eighth century* (usually called First Isaiah) is limited to Isaiah 1–39, because after chapter 39 there is an immense break—literary, historical, and theological—before chapter 40. As soon as we have said that, however, it is clear that the material is much more complex than such a historical connection, for chapters 1–39 contain many other matters as well that are not linked to the eighth century. In any case, this chapter focuses on the middle and final portions of the book of Isaiah that are known as Second Isaiah (chaps. 40–55) and Third Isaiah (chaps. 56–66).

Although anticipated in some passages before chapter 39, there is a long silence in the book of Isaiah after chapter 39. That rhetorical silence corresponds to the long displacement in exile of the leading inhabitants of Jerusalem (see Ps. 137). But then, as the geopolitical world turned against the imperial power of Babylon, the tradition of Isaiah erupted in a new torrent of hopeful imagination in chapter 40 and following. These are not the words of the old prophet from the eighth century BCE; they are, nonetheless, oracles that derived from and remain faithful to the older Isaiah tradition. This poetry bears witness to hope that arises out of the powerful convergence of theological imagination and historical reality, whereby the political reality of a new emergent Persian power is transposed into and understood as the emancipatory action of YHWH.

I. The Holy Way Highway

This new poetry appeals to the imagery of a highway of homecoming in 35:8. That imagery stands at the beginning of the new poetry:

In the wilderness prepare the way of the LORD,
make straight in the desert a highway for our God.

40:3

The poetry imagines Jerusalem joyously filled with hope on its way home, because YHWH has made a new decision about world history. That new decision is called gospel, meaning good news or good tidings. The gospel tells of YHWH's new initiative:

Get you up to a high mountain,
  O Zion, herald of good tidings;
lift up your voice with strength,
  O Jerusalem, herald of good tidings;
  lift it up, do not fear;
say to the cities of Judah,
  "Here is your God!"

40:9

The declaration "Here is your God" is an assertion that after a long season of absence YHWH is back in play. When YHWH takes such an initiative, the imperial power of Babylon and its gods is helpless to resist. In the realpolitik of the time, that newness came to expression as the rise of Persia (Iran) in the east under the leadership of Cyrus, who in Isaiah 45:1 is termed by YHWH as "my messiah." Given that turn in geopolitics and given the new prospects of the Persian Empire, the dislocated persons from Jerusalem are now permitted to go home after a long season of displacement (see 2 Chr. 36:22–23). Thus the poetry reflects changed political circumstance but voices it theologically as a turn in the intent of YHWH.

The task of the poet is to provide his displaced listeners news of the changed theological reality that is reflected in changed political circumstance. No doubt the force of Babylonian rule and the attractiveness of the Babylonian economy had caused many Jews to settle and to regard Babylon as the context for their life and faith. The poet, however, summons his listeners to the joyous and arduous alternative of return to the city of Jerusalem. The poet utilizes a number of rhetorical strategies to recruit his listeners into the prospect of homecoming. A series of "salvation oracles" is issued on behalf of YHWH that tell the people not to fear:

> Do not fear, for I have redeemed you;
> I have called you by name, you are mine.
> 43:1 (see 41:10, 14; 43:5; 44:8)

It was fear of and submission to the power of Babylon that blocked the possibility of discerning YHWH's new resolve in the world. The overcoming of fear, accomplished by articulation of the gospel, was designed to liberate exilic Israel from the grip of imperial ideology, and so to evoke the awareness of and hope in a historical possibility outside the domain of imperial ideology.

The poet imagines a great cosmic courtroom in which there is a trial to determine who the real god is. Babylonian gods are invited to offer evidence of their divinity, that is, their power; but they offer no such evidence (Isa. 41:22–23). The inescapable verdict is that they are nothing, not to be feared, honored, or obeyed (41:24). By contrast, YHWH declares, as evidence of his transformative capacity, that he has "stirred up" Cyrus, the Persian, who has initiated the radical transformation of international politics (41:25). The conclusion to which the poem drives is that those who listen to the poet, exilic Israel, can observe that their submission to Babylon is out of step with reality, because the singularly effective reality is the God who will bring them home.

The poet contrasts the gods of the empire and YHWH, the God of homecoming (chap. 46), in whom we may hope. The imperial gods are shown to be inanimate objects that must be carried as burden (vv. 1–2), whereas YHWH is one who can take concrete action:

> I have made, and I will bear;
> I will carry and will save.
> 46:4

The defeat of the Babylonian gods in chapter 46 is matched in chapter 47 by the defeat and utter humiliation of the nation of Babylon. Thus the poetry, line by line, enacts the debasement of Babylon:

Come down and sit in the dust,
  virgin daughter Babylon!
Sit on the ground without a throne,
  daughter Chaldea!
For you shall no more be called
  tender and delicate.
Take the millstones and grind meal.
47:1–2

The reason for the defeat of Babylon, says the poet, is that Babylon did not "show mercy" (v. 6). Like every superpower, Babylon failed to reckon with the ultimacy of YHWH and so imagined itself to be completely autonomous and free to act as it chose.

A variety of images is used to contrast the dismantling of Babylon with the rehabilitation of Israel and especially of Jerusalem. Thus in chapter 54, in the imagery of divorce and remarriage, Israel had been abandoned by husband YHWH. Now, says the poet, the husband who had abandoned her has redeemed her and restored her to honor as his wife. While the language is indeed patriarchal and attests to the vulnerability of women in that ancient culture, the imagery serves a lyrical purpose to instill hope by acknowledging divine abandonment and the end of abandonment in restoration:

For a brief moment I abandoned you,
  but with great compassion I will gather you.
In overflowing wrath for a moment
  I hid my face from you,
but with everlasting love I will have compassion on you,
  says the LORD, your Redeemer.
54:7–8

The double use of "compassion" suggests YHWH's intensely emotional commitment to Israel.

The sum of all this poetry is to assert a new intention on the part of YHWH that is voiced in the term "gospel":

How beautiful on the mountains
  are the feet of the messenger who announces peace,
who brings *good news*,

who announces salvation,
who says to Zion, "Your God reigns."

                                                    52:7

This poetic performance in the midst of dislocated persons is an invitation to perceive historical circumstance differently and to hope. While they had succumbed to imperial ideology, they could not imagine homecoming, because Babylon would never permit it. When they were able to imagine outside that ideology, however, they could see that the empire is not a given. The empire is an ideological construct that will be interrupted and trumped by the counternews of the gospel that asserts an alternative reality. In the end the poet envisions and enacts, before the very eyes of the dislocated, a great procession of homecoming to Jerusalem. Jerusalem will indeed be marching to freedom in the light of God! It will be a grand public procession in broad daylight:

For you shall go out in joy,
    and be led back in peace;
the mountains and the hills before you
    shall burst into song,
    and all the trees of the field shall clap their hands.
                              55:12 (see 52:11–12)

The faithful are always departing the grip of imperial ideology!

II. Israel to Be a Servant to All

This grand and glorious vision, however, is interrupted by the countertheme of servanthood. In several poetic units, Israel is reminded that its emancipation has a vocation larger than its own homecoming:

I have given you as a covenant to the people,
    a light to the nations,
    to open the eyes that are blind,
to bring out the prisoners from the dungeon,
    from the prison those who sit in darkness.
                              42:6b–7 (see 49:6)

The precise meaning of these lines is not clear. It is clear enough, however, to see that the future of Israel places Israel on the horizon of other peoples. Israel is to be a vehicle or an instrument through which YHWH is to relate in a covenantal way to other nations. That notion of servanthood, however, is greatly intensified in the difficult poem of 52:13–53:12, wherein Israel, as God's servant,

> . . . was wounded for our transgressions,
>   crushed for our iniquities;
> upon him was the punishment that made us whole,
>   and by his bruises we are healed.
>
> 53:5

The poem affirms that this one may bear suffering for another, meaning not only the suffering of Israel but also the suffering of the world. This notion of course is expressed in poetic idiom and offers no theory or explanation about how this may happen. We are not told how that suffering may heal others. It is to be recognized, of course, that Christians have taken up the poem with reference to Jesus, who as the Christ bears the sin of the world and is a covenant to other peoples. Without in any way rejecting that reading of the poetry, it is important to recognize that this poem has long been read in a different way that takes the people Israel as the servant who bears the sin of the world. It is not, in my judgment, necessary to choose between these readings but rather to recognize that the poem is open enough to permit such readings that turn out to be parallel readings by Jews and by Christians. Both readings hope in an agent of God who transforms the suffering of the world.

III. Third Isaiah

The third section of the book of Isaiah comprises chapters 56–66, which for reasons now obvious are termed by scholars Third Isaiah. It is the judgment of most scholars that this material reflects a community occupied with issues very different from those in chapters 40–55, and so it is judged to be a later literature. The apparent context of this literature is after the return and restoration anticipated in Second Isaiah, in a context where the community had to work out disputed internal questions of social life and religious practice. It is common to locate this literature somewhere between the building of the Second Temple (520–516), on which see Haggai and Zechariah, and the restoration of Ezra and Nehemiah after 450 BCE. Most scholars prefer a date earlier rather than later, thus soon after 520. That date is not very long after the hypothetical date of Second Isaiah, but places the literature in a very different sociohistorical circumstance.

Whereas Second Isaiah is preoccupied with emancipation from Babylon, Third Isaiah is concerned with internal communal life and the tensions that must have arisen among the parties that we might label "liberal" and "conservative." If we accept chapters 56–66 as a reflection of the work and discipline of reformulation, we notice that this poetry begins with a resolve about social justice:

> Thus says the LORD:
>   Maintain justice, and do what is right,
> for soon my salvation will come,
>   and my deliverance be revealed.
> 56:1

Justice would seem to be a leading motif of the whole, so that the work of the developing community is to guarantee socioeconomic justice.

> [T]here is no justice in their paths. . . .
> [J]ustice is far from us. . . .
> We wait for justice. . . .
> Justice is turned back. . . .
> 59:8–9, 11, 14

The concrete implementation of justice is the work of the restored community that is evident in a series of texts:

My House Shall Be Called a House of Prayer for All Peoples (Isa. 56:7)

In chapter 56 there is a contest over who is eligible for membership in the community. Isaiah 56:7 affirms that foreigners who do not have clear Jewish pedigree and eunuchs are seen to have no barrier to inclusion. Thus the text urges inclusiveness and flies in the face of the restrictions of Ezra, who wants to limit membership in restored

Israel to those of "holy seed"—of proper genealogy (Ezra 9:2). This text likely offers a vision that was taken up in the early church with the much-contested inclusion of Gentiles.

Is Not This the Fast I Choose? (Isa. 58:6)

In chapter 58 there is a dispute concerning proper worship. In the familiar part of that text, it is stated that the proper fast, the most intense of religious disciplines, is

> . . . to share your bread with the hungry,
>   and bring the homeless poor into your house;
> when you see the naked, to cover them,
>   and not to hide yourself from your own kin.
>   58:7

In this interpretation, worship is transposed into neighborly engagement. We usually do not notice that in verses 1–4 there is a critique of worship that is a satisfying of religious desire but that is compartmentalized; such worship may go along with "oppress[ion of] all your workers" (58:3). Such worship is cut off from the neighborly life of the community. Taken as a whole, this poem offers a sharp contrast between self-indulgent worship and an alternative that has love of neighbor in purview.

The Spirit of the Lord GOD Is upon Me (Isa. 61:1)

In the familiar text of chapter 61, the one who speaks is again given a vocation by the spirit of the Lord to act in transformative ways in society. Reference to "the year of the LORD's favor" (v. 2) leads to the likelihood that what is intended here is nothing less than an observance of the year of jubilee (see Lev. 25), a ritual enactment of neighborliness whereby neighborliness prevails over sharp economic practice.

This sustained focus on justice is expressed through *inclusiveness* (Isa. 56), *neighborly worship* (chap. 58), and *economic transformation* (chap. 61). In sum, the poetry offers a vision of a new Jerusalem (65:17–25) in which we may hope. This is no longer the old Jerusalem of the eighth century, which failed the test of justice and righteousness. This is no longer the Jerusalem that was grieved by Babylonian dislocation. Rather, this is buoyant poetry that offers the imagination and perspective of a new Jerusalem that is intended by God, one that is permeated with neighborly governance and economic solidarity, supported by the attentiveness of God's own self. This hope-filled poetry anticipates a new urban economy for Jerusalem in which there are no infant mortality (65:20), no foreclosures on homes (vv. 21–22), and no children at risk (v. 23), but full protection in an infrastructure of caring justice.

IV. Conclusion

The book of Isaiah, in a complex way over a long period of time, is a great lyrical articulation of a city that is *humiliated* in deep failure and then is *exalted* in glorious, possible well-being. In the midst of Third Isaiah, one might give special attention to chapters 60–62, which voice a lyrical power that compares favorably with that of Second Isaiah. These chapters in grand lyrical fashion anticipate future well-being for Israel. These chapters include familiar formulations, most especially 61:1–4, which is reiterated in Luke 4:18–19:

> The spirit of the Lord GOD is upon me,
>   because the LORD has anointed me;
> he has sent me to bring good news to the oppressed,
>   to bind up the brokenhearted,
> to proclaim liberty to the captives,
>   and release to the prisoners;
> to proclaim the year of the LORD's favor,
>   and the day of vengeance of our God;
> to comfort all who mourn;
> to provide for those who mourn in Zion—
>   to give them a garland instead of ashes,
> the oil of gladness instead of mourning,
>   the mantle of praise instead of a faint spirit.
> They will be called oaks of righteousness,
>   the planting of the LORD, to display his glory.
> They shall build up the ancient ruins,
>   they shall raise up the former devastations;

they shall repair the ruined cities,
the devastations of many generations.

Isa. 61:1–4

Beyond these expectations, the lyrical promise of 65:17–25 voices the most sweeping anticipation of the "new age" when YHWH's rule is fully established, a promise that is the basis for the immense and final promise of the New Testament in Revelation 21: "Then I saw a new heaven and a new earth; for the first heaven and the first earth had passed away, and the sea was no more. And I saw the holy city, the new Jerusalem, coming down out of heaven from God, prepared as a bride adorned for her husband" (Rev. 21:1–2).

While the cosmic scope of "new heaven and a new earth" is the furthest reach of biblical hope, along with them is the promise of a "new Jerusalem" that will be ordered by YHWH's presence in terms of justice, compassion, and neighborliness. The culmination of the book of Isaiah with "new Jerusalem" (Isa. 65:17–25; see 66:10–13 as well) brings closure to the Jerusalem theme that dominates the entire book of Isaiah. Thus First Isaiah, in sum, bespeaks the destruction of Jerusalem as the judgment of YHWH; Second Isaiah anticipates restoration of Jerusalem; Third Isaiah struggles with the shaping of the Jerusalem to come. The sequence of First, Second, and Third Isaiah attracts the interpreted memory of Jerusalem as *destroyed*, *expected*, and *reorganized*. The traditioning process thus has ordered material into a coherent interpretive pattern that has risen out of, and with respect to, many different circumstances. Having noted the sequence of First, Second, and Third Isaiah, however, it is equally important to notice that in the final form of the book an overture articulates all these themes at the very outset:

How the faithful city
    has become a whore!
    She that was full of justice,
righteousness lodged in her—
    but now murderers!
Your silver has become dross,
    your wine is mixed with water.
Your princes are rebels
    and companions of thieves.

Everyone loves a bribe
   and runs after gifts.
They do not defend the orphan,
   and the widow's cause does not come before them.

Therefore says the Sovereign, the LORD of hosts, the Mighty One
      of Israel:
Ah, I will pour out my wrath on my enemies,
   and avenge myself on my foes!
I will turn my hand against you;
   I will smelt away your dross as with lye
   and remove all your alloy.
And I will restore your judges as at the first,
   and your counselors as at the beginning.
Afterward you shall be called the city of righteousness,
   the faithful city.

Zion shall be redeemed by justice,
   and those in her who repent, by righteousness.
                                                    1:21–27

This brief précis traces the entire history of Jerusalem as it is to
be lined out in what follows in the book. The entire book of Isaiah concerns YHWH's love-hate relationship with Jerusalem, a city
punished by YHWH in anger and then (but not until then) loved to
newness by this same YHWH.

We must read Isaiah first of all as an authentic report on the vagaries of the history of the city all the way from the glory of David and
Solomon to the restored, more modest city of Judaism. It is a Jewish
book about this contested Jewish city that is the pivot point of messianic expectation.

It is clear that in our belated reading of the book as Christians,
we have found it, more than any other book of the Old Testament,
to be a lively testimony to the claims of Jesus as the Messiah. The
early church did not focus on the dramatic whole of the book. Rather,
it found texts that were peculiarly illuminating to the life of Jesus
and to the church. On the one hand, the dismissiveness of 6:9–10 is
quoted in each Gospel narrative as a justification for the way Jews
have failed to be fully God's people (Matt. 13:14–15; Mark 4:12;
Luke 8:10; John 12:40). On the other hand, the royal oracle of 9:2–7

is found to concern King Jesus, and the poem about saving through being wounded turns out to be a fitting text for understanding the passion narrative of Jesus (see Acts 8:32–33).

Beyond the historical reading of Jewish memory and the christological reading of the church, we may also, in our own circumstance, see the lyrical sum of the book of Isaiah as an illumination of our lived reality in the United States and in the West. I have come to think that, as the destruction of Jerusalem is the critical icon of Old Testament loss and hope, so 9/11 is the critical icon of loss and hope in our society. Given that provisional equivalence, it is possible for us to read the book of Isaiah, albeit belatedly, as an interpretation of our contemporary drama of loss and displacement and anticipated possibility. The book of Isaiah goes deep into the abyss of loss, grief, absence, and abandonment, as does our life around 9/11. The book reaches hopefully into the future after the displacement, as we might after 9/11. That future, as the book of Isaiah knew, is partly divine gift and partly human work. That work depends on imagining an alternative in poetic ways, exactly what the book of Isaiah does.

Homiletical Focus: "Pregnant with Possibility"*

The story of the people of God in the Old Testament ends in failure: disappointment, destruction, disaster, displacement, despair. (That is all the hard words that begin with *d* that I could muster!) The city of Jerusalem and its temple and the monarchy there were all terminated. The leadership was deported to be refugees in a foreign land.

I

Then, in an inexplicable explosion of hope-filled poetry, the book of Isaiah runs toward its end with three wondrous chapters of prophetic

---

*Editor's note: What follows is a sermon based primarily on the hope-filled poetry of Isaiah, which Brueggemann preached on January 17, 2016, MLK holiday weekend. The lectionary texts for the day were Isaiah 62:1–5; Psalm 36:5–10; 1 Corinthians 12:1–11; John 2:1–11.

imagination. You may not recognize them, but you are perhaps familiar with them:

- In chapter 60, "Arise, shine; for your light has come" (v. 1), a good Epiphany text;
- In chapter 61, "The spirit of the Lord GOD is upon me" (v. 1);
- In chapter 62, our text, God says: "For Zion's sake I will not keep silent[!]" (v. 1).

The silence of despair is about to be broken by God! These three chapters together constitute a massive declaration—given without justification or explanation—that there will be a new beginning for Israel. The grip of failure and despair is broken by this awesome buoyant poetry. There will be a new Jerusalem, a new temple, a new covenant, a new beginning.

II

In our text, chapter 62, a great epiphany is coming:

For Zion's sake I will not keep silent,
    and for Jerusalem's sake I will not rest,
until her vindication shines out like the dawn,
    and her salvation like a burning torch.
                                    62:1

Then, near the end of our reading, the poet gives us three images to contradict old failures with new possibilities:

- "You shall no more be termed Forsaken . . . but you shall be called My Delight Is in Her" (v. 4). The imagery is of a failed marriage in which the woman, in a patriarchal society, is abandoned because she is barren. But now she is restored to well-being, because her husband takes delight in her. The move is from abandonment to delight.
- The second image is that "your land shall no more be termed Desolate. . ." (which in a patriarchal society means you have no children), but now "Married" (v. 4), capable of bearing children, the deep joy of new birth.
- In a third image Jerusalem will be like a bride with a rejoicing bridegroom; the newness will be like a wedding party (v. 5).

These three images are of a new young love that brings joy, a total contradiction of present failure. We can dwell in these images, even when we recognize that gender-wise they are one-sided and quite patriarchal.

I want to comment on the second of these images:

Desolate . . . no children . . . barren

and then

Married!

You have perhaps heard of the old Canaanite god Baal. That is the god of agriculture who was said to bring rain and cause crops to flourish. In our verse—a little technical grammar—the word "married," that is, made fruitful and joyous, is the *feminine passive participle* of Baal, "she who has been made fruitful," or "she who has been made pregnant." The name of Baal has been declined so that the feminine passive participle for Baal is *Beulah land*; the land that was empty and savaged by war has been made generative and productive and flourishing. The right translation of the term is "pregnant," but the very proper translation committee could not say "pregnant," but settled for "married," capable of children.

So imagine: the poet addresses this helpless, hopeless, barren people who are displaced refugees, and declares, "*Your land is pregnant*," your history is pregnant with new possibility. You are loaded with new futures. It is no wonder that we get the joyous imagery of bride and bridegroom and a wedding party. All Israel could sing and dance about new possibility. And God can sing and dance with them for new possibility.

III

The scene changes in our Gospel reading. But Jesus is also at a wedding party. This one is no different—dancing and singing, and no doubt joking about having many children. And Jesus is working the crowd. He changes everything, as he always does. He changes water into wine. He intrudes into the party with deep newness. John calls his act a "sign." New wine, given inexplicably, is a sign of the power of Jesus to bring newness. The wedding is a sign of new futures.

Maybe, like many brides even today, she may have been pregnant by the time of the party. Jesus hosts a party of new history that cannot be held in old wineskins. He makes all things new!

IV

Isn't that exactly what Dr. King was doing as we remember him today? He lived and worked in a similar setting of displacement, disaster, and despair. Slavery had made a huge population to be refugees in their own land. And there he is, a poet like Isaiah: "I have a dream!" Isaiah had imagined a new heaven, a new earth, a new Jerusalem, a new temple. Jesus imagined a new kingdom, a new political-economic arrangement that could not be contained in old patterns of social power. Martin dreamed us all tougher in dignity and justice, even at Stone Mountain and many less ominous places as well. Isaiah and Jesus and Martin all urged us to newness that deeply contradicts all the old ways that we treasure:

- Isaiah: welcome to *Beulah land*, a land pregnant with possibility.
- Jesus: *new wine*, the wine of the kingdom of God, the new neighborliness that does economic justice for all.
- Martin: *a dream of a nation* that practiced its creed of economic justice for all, along with liberty for all.

All these bold witnesses testify to pregnant possibility that is as sure as God is sure. The social upheaval all around us may indeed be birth pangs of that dream pushing its way out to new life.

V

Is that sufficient for us? Are we among the deportees who live as displaced refugees? Are you among the displaced who believe our setting has no way to the future? Are you a carrier of anxiety about the future that immobilizes you? Or are you a practitioner of fatigue that distorts your best self? If you are any of these, then this is a word for you. A word has been uttered that is life-changing:

- a word by Isaiah about pregnancy

- a word by Jesus about new wine
- a word by Martin about a dream

They all speak about a pregnancy, a loaded possibility of being born again, beyond despair, brought home to celebrate a new life together.

So ponder that you and I are at this moment when newness kicks in like a fetus kicking toward birth:

- Newness kicks in when Isaiah moves us from desolation to married.
- Newness kicks in when Jesus in that awesome moment gives us new wine.
- Newness kicks in when Martin defies old reality with God's intention.

We are on the receiving end. But we have to receive. We are on the receiving end of the new pregnancy of history,

- in a political economy that has failed;
- in a society of anxiety that wants us to play safe and private;
- in a world of violence that seems endless.

We could give in to the despair. We could withdraw and hope to be safe in our small world of control. We could engage in nostalgia and yearn for the good old days that are gone. But the gospel is otherwise. The gospel is the excitement of new pregnancy. And we can welcome it. Among the most awesome words spoken in intimacy are "I'm pregnant." Sometimes it is hard news, most often glad news. For us this is glad news. It is glad news that our history is loaded with possibility. We can dance and sing. And we can act.

Isaiah moves his poem along with a series of imperatives:

Go through, go through the gates,
    prepare the way for the people;
build up, build up the highway,
    clear it of stones,
    lift up an ensign over the peoples.
62:10

The poem culminates like a pregnancy coming to fruition:

> They shall be called, "The Holy People,
>   The Redeemed of the LORD";
> and you shall be called, "Sought Out,
>   A City Not Forsaken."
>
> v. 12

Imagine new historical possibility, new action, new freedom, new responsibility, new joy together beyond fear:

The Holy People (that's us!),
The Redeemed of the Lord (all of us!),
Sought Out (not abandoned or forgotten!),
A City Not Forsaken (this city, our city!).

No more despair; because God calls us to act from our new birthright, right here, right now! Think of this well-beloved city, divided east and west, and now a city not forsaken!

Questions for Reflection

1. Isaiah, through poetry, evokes the idea of homecoming in the minds and hearts of readers. YHWH has returned from a long absence and opened up a way home for the people of Israel. Have you ever felt abandoned by God or absent from home? How did God show up again and lead you home?

2. Brueggemann distinguishes the biblical God of homecoming from the idols that were the Babylonian gods of empire. What are the idols in your own life? What do you carry with you that are only burdens, or that elicit fear?

3. Justice is a central theme in the words of Third Isaiah. Brueggemann explains that the work of the community is to guarantee socio-economic justice through inclusion, neighborly engagement, and economic transformation. In what ways can you engage in these practices, within yourself and in your community?

4. Brueggemann calls us to imagine new historical possibilities in our world, characterized by new actions, freedoms, and joys beyond all fears. How do you take up this imaginative call? What do you imagine the new well-beloved city being like?

PART FOUR

The Writings: Hope of Transformation

Chapter 7

Hope Transformed in the Writings

Exegetical Focus (Daniel 2–4)

*T*he third canon of the Hebrew Bible is termed the Writings. The term most likely reflects (a) an awareness that Judaism had devolved to scroll making in a context where it was peculiarly vulnerable, and (b) a recognition that the primal scroll makers are scribes who preserve old traditions and interpret them by way of commentary. The nomenclature "Writings" itself goes far to characterize the Judaism that is reflected in this third canon, which has a miscellaneous quality to it. The most accessible (if somewhat rambling) discussion of this issue is by Donn Morgan.[1] His discussion revolves around three points that are worth notice.

1. What I have termed the "miscellaneous" character of the collection Morgan rightly understands as *pluralism*. The third canon consists in a pluralism of genre, topic, and perspective befitting the pluralistic character of Judaism. The older view of Second Temple Judaism, perhaps especially favored by Christians, tended to think of a "normative Judaism" that revolved around Ezra's preoccupation with the Torah—thus a Judaism that Christians could treat dismissively in terms of the "Law." Against such an uninformed reductionism, it is now clear that Judaism in and through the period of the rise of Christianity was a vibrant, complex interpretive community, so that the only way in which Judaism of the period could designate Holy Writings was bound to embody pluralism.[2] Thus the collection is something of an ecumenical achievement, a big-tent enactment of Judaism.

2. Morgan helpfully shows that the writings are in dialogic continuity with the older traditions of the Torah and the Prophets. Indeed,

this *dialogic continuity* with the older traditions is important, for Morgan concludes that the valuing of older traditions is all that the several books of the Writings have in common.[3]

3. As the Writings are in dialogue with the older, more basic traditions, so the Writings are in dialogue with cultural-historical context as well. It is important to recognize that the exile and the termination of Israelite political independence, the resulting Diaspora of Jews, and the encircling cultural hegemony of the Greeks after the hegemony of the Persians left the Jewish community in a fragmented situation. In that context, immense courage and interpretive flexibility were required in order to sustain Jewish canonical coherence and identity, the task of sustenance undertaken in many ways by many subcommunities.[4]

Thus *pluralism, dialogue with tradition,* and *dialogue with context* help to provide an integrated perspective on this literature. My own way of seeing this pluralism whole is to suggest four textual groupings in the material:

a. The three great books of Psalms, Job, and Proverbs together constitute a sustained liturgical-sapiential reflection on God-given order in the world and the inescapable posing of the question of theodicy, to which Israel gives faithful answer in hymn and lament.

b. The Five Scrolls, or the Megilloth (Song of Songs/Song of Solomon, Ruth, Lamentations, Ecclesiastes/Qoheleth, Esther), evidence the way in which various voices of the community were drawn into the liturgical calendar. For in the end it is the liturgical calendar that will provide socialization into and sustenance of a distinctive community.[5]

c. The apocalyptic book of Daniel perhaps reflects a compromise whereby, from a great plentitude of apocalyptic texts that were available, the canonizing tradition was able to exclude from the sacred books all but this apocalyptic book (and the latter part of Zechariah). It is clear that the book of Daniel, in canonical form, is the quintessential book of hope in the Hebrew Bible, hope that invites courage and freedom in the enactment of a singularly Jewish identity. Thus, as the books of Psalms, Job, and Proverbs pose the question of theodicy, the book of Daniel is a characteristic voice of hope that is totally sure of YHWII's triumph over all threats to Jerusalem and all threats that would dismantle the world of YHWH's creation. Thus the focus of this chapter and the next on the book of Daniel.

d. This third canon ends by a presentation of the historical books of Ezra, Nehemiah, and Chronicles. But of course they are not "history" in any modern sense of the term, any more than the Deuteronomic History, a text that is a predecessor to the Chronicles, is "history." The four books of Ezra, Nehemiah, and 1 and 2 Chronicles represent a theological-ideological insistence for a particular shape and mode of Judaism; it is important to recognize, however, that as powerful as that advocacy is, it did not and was not able to claim the field in the third canon, for its advocacy is placed alongside the other advocacies already mentioned. It is of particular interest that, taken historically, Ezra and Nehemiah should follow Chronicles, as is evident in the overlap and reiteration of Ezra 1:2–3 from 2 Chronicles 36:23. The inversion of the sequence from what we might have expected is apparently so that the third canon, and thus the entire Hebrew Bible, can end with the edict of Cyrus the Persian, with its project of a return from exile (2 Chr. 36:22–23). Thus the canon ends with an expected recovery, for Judaism—with its preoccupation with exile—is always returning home again, always yet again recovering YHWH's promise of the land, always again working beneath the radar of imperial hegemony according to its own distinctive identity.

These four groupings, then, evidence Judaism at work in a variety of ways, coming to terms with and finding new hope in its circumstance. By many acts of imagination Judaism comes to terms with a necessary flexibility; in the end, however, it finally never yields the core of its theological identity. Jack Miles has observed that by the end of the third canon, the God of Israel is for the most part silent and absent.[6] But then, given that silence and absence, everything for this God depends upon the answering of Israel. The third canon is an answer whereby the community is sustained and YHWH is kept available in a community that has become politically marginal but confessionally resolved and sure of the will and identity that belongs to it in a dangerous circumstance. The answer turns out to be revelatory of this God who is offered according to the resolve given in the answer of Israel.

I

The book of Daniel is often disregarded because of its bizarre, enig-matic "apocalyptic" dimension. But the first half of the book, my focus, offers narratives that are not apocalyptic but are dramatically alive in agonistic ways. The antagonist for Daniel in this narra-tive is Nebuchadnezzar, a reference point that situates Daniel in the Babylonian Empire, where Jews were displaced and required to sing the songs of Zion in a strange land. In what is a litmus test for critical scholarship, the book of Daniel is commonly placed in the period of Antiochus, the Syrian heir to Alexander the Great, who brought with him an aggressive Hellenistic perspective that sought to override local traditions, including the traditions of Juda-ism. In that context, the book of Daniel offers a mode of faith that is aware of but not very hopeful about the violent resistance of the Maccabees, who are discounted in the book as only a "little help" (Dan. 11:34).

Whether we take the proposed Babylonian context or the critical Hellenistic context, either way the Daniel narratives concern a crisis of Judaism when Jews were marginalized, and when the peculiar tradition and identity of Judaism were under assault from a large, hegemonic power. The wonder of the Daniel narrative is that this threatened Jew and his company did not withdraw from hegemonic society in order to nurture and maintain an alternative distinct iden-tity. Rather, Daniel is perforce a quite public man in the narrative, boldly playing an assertive part in maintaining a particular presence in the affairs of that hegemonic society.

John Collins concludes that the purpose of such a Diaspora hero as Daniel is to offer sustaining, hope-filled literature in order

(1) to remind the Jews that their monotheistic religion is a glori-ous heritage infinitely superior to the paganism with its gross idol worship; (2) to encourage the Jews to remain loyal to that heritage like the outstanding protagonists of the book who were willing to risk their social, economic, and political status and even their lives by steadfastly refusing to compromise their faith, and (3) to show dramatically and imaginatively that the God of Israel comes to the rescue and delivers those who believe in him despite even the severest reverses, including death by martyrdom.[7]

Concerning faith lived in the Diaspora, Daniel Smith concludes,

> If Daniel, Esther, and Joseph are examples of exilic hero stories, designed didactically to advise a "lifestyle for the diaspora," then the hero, as Abrahams, Meinhold, and Collins emphasized, is a focus for a group: one in whom hopes are placed and one who provides an example as well. It is significant that the result of virtually all the diaspora hero stories is a change of condition, either implied or explicitly stated, for the Jewish people as a whole. Thus, Jewish diaspora hero stories become deliverer stories as well.[8]

Smith, following the work of N. H. H. Graburn, proposes that displaced people, those who are powerless in their own land, are living in "the Fourth World," in order to maintain identity when the dominant culture is bent on marginalizing—if not crushing—that identity:

> The alternative worldview presented in this study could be called a "Fourth World" perspective. In modern sociological literature, exiled peoples have come to be included among those otherwise collectively known as "the Fourth World." Graburn's definition of the Fourth World provides a helpful beginning:
>
>> All aboriginal or native peoples whose lands fall within the national boundaries and techno-bureaucratic administrations of the countries of the first, second, and third worlds. As such, they are peoples without countries of their own, peoples who are usually in the minority, and without the power to direct the course of their collective lives.[9]

In what follows, I propose, mutatis mutandis, that the Daniel narrative may be a resource for the church in the midst of the national security state in the United States. I am aware that that is a huge mutatis mutandis, but I believe it is an accurate description of our situation of faith and ministry. For all the religious talk among us, it is the case that the dominant ideology of our culture, which I term "military consumerism"—an ideology that totalizes much of the imagination of both conservatives and liberals—is profoundly inimical to the primal claims of the gospel.

Thus our context is not unlike that of the early church in the book of Acts, wherein proclamation of resurrection was a sufficient reason to be summoned before the authorities. I will work with that analogue, even though one must not press it too far. I believe that a faithful and hopeful response to the gospel for the sake of the world may begin in a recognition of our true place in that world. And I judge that our evangelical claims are in deep contradiction to the claims of the global empire that is our societal habitat.

Thus, I propose this analogue: Daniel's work is to practice his Jewish identity in generative ways in an alien hegemony, to protect that identity, and to impinge upon that hegemony in transformative ways. The church's work is to practice our baptismal identity in generative ways in an alien hegemony, to protect our baptismal identity, and to impinge upon that hegemony in transformative ways.

II

I will consider three narratives of confrontation in the book of Daniel, with particular attention to the third one. I will be partly interested in the conduct and utterance of Daniel, because he is the key "Fourth World" figure amid the dominant world wherein he finds himself.

1. In the long narrative of Daniel 2, Nebuchadnezzar, a cipher for the ancient and for the contemporary national security state, has a disturbing dream that is propelled by the impingement of the holy truth upon an otherwise hermetically sealed system. The "magicians" of the empire, the intelligence community, are required by Nebuchadnezzar not only to interpret the dream but to tell the dream. But they cannot! In his frustration with his own intelligence apparatus, Nebuchadnezzar decrees that all of them should be executed.

In the midst of a hegemonic violent rage comes Daniel, carrier of a distinct faith identity, a man with "prudence and discretion." In preparation for his work, Daniel

- urges his companions to pray for mercy for himself and for the imperial wise men (Dan. 2:17–18);
- offers a doxology to the God of heaven, praise to God for sovereign power and wisdom (vv. 20–23); and
- urges that the lives of the imperial magicians be spared (v. 24).

These three actions taken altogether amount to a vigorous intervention in the world of Nebuchadnezzar and reflect deep rootage in Jewish tradition concerning mercy, wisdom, and divine power.

In verses 25–45, Daniel reiterates the dream and gives its interpretation. It is about the rise and fall of great empires, including that of Nebuchadnezzar. This is a formidable philosophy of history that reflects the world of the late Persian and early Hellenistic periods, all of which pertains to YHWH's rule. Daniel allows himself two claims for his distinct faith and hope.

First, he asserts that it is the God of heaven who knows the mysteries that he is about to disclose:

> [T]here is a God in heaven who reveals mysteries, and he has disclosed to King Nebuchadnezzar what will happen at the end of days. Your dream and the visions of your head as you lay in bed were these. . . . But as for me, this mystery has not been revealed to me because of any wisdom that I have more than any other living being, but in order that the interpretation may be known to the king and that you may understand the thoughts of your mind. (Dan. 2:28, 30)

The coming course of events is beyond the ken of the empire that imagined its own unchallengeable sovereignty. There is a plan beyond worldly power that is carried by Daniel.

Second, there is coming a rule that will supersede all human pretensions:

> And in the days of those kings the God of heaven will set up a kingdom that shall never be destroyed, nor shall this kingdom be left to another people. It shall crush all these kingdoms and bring them to an end, and it shall stand forever. (2:44)

The upshot of this narrative is a remarkable one. Given such assurance, Nebuchadnezzar turns out to be benign. Daniel has tamed the violent rage of the empire with his larger, hope-filled perspective on the coming governance of the God of heaven. Nebuchadnezzar for an instant issues a doxology to the God of Daniel:

> The king said to Daniel, "Truly, your God is God of gods and Lord of kings and a revealer of mysteries, for you have been able to reveal this mystery!" (2:47)

Daniel himself, as response to his exhibit of bold courage, is presented to the king and given many gifts. Without interpretive comment, the narrative has shown how it is that Daniel the Jew emerges, by his bold wisdom, with transformative impact on the empire. And his God is praised by the empire!

2. In the second narrative, chapter 3, the relationship of Daniel to Nebuchadnezzar—that is, Jew to empire, local identity in the face of hegemonic power—is much more aggressive and violent. In this narrative, Nebuchadnezzar now has the self-aggrandizing statue before which all shall bow down. The action to follow is situated in appropriate state liturgy:

> Therefore, as soon as all the peoples heard the sound of the horn, pipe, lyre, trigon, harp, drum, and entire musical ensemble, all the peoples, nations, and languages fell down and worshiped the golden statue that King Nebuchadnezzar had set up. (3:7)

All of that worked smoothly, and it was in any case just liturgy. But such a hegemonic power has an immense and effective surveillance system. It did not take long before Nebuchadnezzar got a report: "[C]ertain Chaldeans came forward and denounced the Jews" (v. 8):

> There are certain Jews whom you have appointed over the affairs of the province of Babylon: Shadrach, Meshach, and Abednego. These pay no heed to you, O king. They do not serve your gods and they do not worship the golden statue that you have set up. (3:12)

It mattered in that ancient world, as now, in what liturgy one participates. After all, even back in Egypt, all that was asked was "Let my people go, so that they may worship me" (e.g., Exod. 7:16). The management of a liturgical system is a life-and-death matter for the maintenance of public power. For that reason, Jewish passive resistance to imperial liturgy immediately evoked imperial aggressiveness:

> Then Nebuchadnezzar in furious rage commanded that Shadrach, Meshach, and Abednego be brought in; so they brought those men before the king. . . . "Now if you are ready when you hear the sound of the horn, pipe, lyre, trigon, harp, drum, and entire musical ensemble to fall down and worship the statue that I have made, well and good. But if you do not worship, you shall immediately

be thrown into a furnace of blazing fire, and who is the god that will deliver you out of my hands?" (3:13, 15)

It seemed innocuous enough. Join the liturgy, and then go home and be an absent Jew. But these Jews could not hide their particular identity. They could not withdraw to safe practice. And so the Jews respond to hegemonic power with a simple but comprehensive refusal:

> Shadrach, Meshach, and Abednego answered the king, "O Nebuchadnezzar, we have no need to present a defense to you in this matter. If our God whom we serve is able to deliver us from the furnace of blazing fire and out of your hand, O king, let him deliver us. But if not, be it known to you, O king, that we will not serve your gods and we will not worship the golden statue that you have set up." (3:16–18)

The answer is a double "if" concerning both eventualities:

> If we are delivered . . . ,
> If we are not delivered . . .

Either way, we will not worship. We will not serve. We will not concede our identity. A great deal is staked on the delivering power of "our God." But not everything is staked on divine intervention. The rest is staked on Jewish stubbornness, on Jewish identity even when miracles are lacking. The remarkable statement is a profound act of defiance. And the threat of the furnace surely draws an allusion back to the exodus deliverance in Deuteronomy:

> But the LORD has taken you and brought you out of the iron-smelter, out of Egypt, to become a people of his very own possession, as you are now. (Deut. 4:20)

This has all happened before, and we are ready and resolved as it happens this time.

The rest of the narrative is history, or legend, or imagination, or whatever. Nebuchadnezzar is yet again in a rage (Dan. 3:19). The maintenance of absolute power that lacks any persuasive legitimacy keeps people edgy, nervous, and prone to violence. The furnace is heated up seven times (3:19). In an oppressive hegemony, every act must be performed in hyperbole. How else to implement "shock and awe"? But as we expect, the courageous, defiant friends are endorsed by the God of all asbestos:

> And the satraps, the prefects, the governors, and the king's counselors gathered together and saw that the fire had not had any power over the bodies of those men; the hair of their heads was not singed, their tunics were not harmed, and not even the smell of fire came from them. (Dan. 3:27)

Even Nebuchadnezzar, slow learner that he is, gets the point and breaks out yet again in doxology:

> Blessed be the God of Shadrach, Meshach, and Abednego, who has sent his angel and delivered his servants who trusted in him. They disobeyed the king's command and yielded up their bodies rather than serve and worship any god except their own God. (3:28)

Nebuchadnezzar sees exactly what has happened. Not unlike Pharaoh, he is a late learner. But he learns. By courageous defiance and testimony, so the narrator attests, even hegemonic power can come to see the truth that subverts all phony claims to authority. The outcome is a decree that the God of Jews must not be disregarded:

> Therefore I make a decree: Any people, nation, or language that utters blasphemy against the God of Shadrach, Meshach, and Abednego shall be torn limb from limb, and their houses laid in ruins; for there is no other god who is able to deliver in this way. (3:29)

"There is no other god who is able to deliver in this way." That is the judgment of the empire! It is no wonder that the Jews are promoted in the imperial government (3:30).

3. The third narrative, chapter 4, moves in the same pattern, again featuring Nebuchadnezzar versus Daniel in a way that subverts the absolute claims of the global reach of Babylon. As this narrative goes, Nebuchadnezzar is in a better mood. He sings to the Most High God (Dan. 4:2–3). Not unlike the psalmist—"I shall never be moved" (Ps. 30:6)—he declares his prosperous ease: "I, Nebuchadnezzar, was living at ease in my home and prospering in my palace" (Dan. 4:4). But the prosperity belongs only to the daylight. At night, when one's guard is down, other stuff happens

to Nebuchadnezzar beyond his favorite construal: "I saw a dream that frightened me; my fantasies in bed and the visions of my head terrified me" (Dan. 4:5).

Nebuchadnezzar now knows what to do, having learned from the events recounted in chapter 2. His own interpreters fail, but he knows about the Jews who can probe the mysteries:

> At last Daniel came in before me—he who was named Belteshazzar after the name of my god, and who is endowed with a spirit of the holy gods—and I told him the dream. (Dan. 4:8)

Nebuchadnezzar even recognizes Daniel's special gifts from God and asks these interpretive gifts to serve the empire:

> O Belteshazzar, chief of the magicians, I know that you are endowed with a spirit of the holy gods and that no mystery is too difficult for you. Hear the dream that I saw; tell me its interpretation. (4:9)

Nebuchadnezzar then tells the dream to Daniel; in contrast to chapter 2, Daniel does not need to recount the dream, only provide the interpretation. The dream is about a luxurious tree that fails. Mindful of the risk he takes in truth-telling, Daniel proceeds in a way not unlike that of Nathan before David: "It is you, O king." It is you who will be brought low, made to eat grass, humiliated, made powerless, "until you have learned that the Most High has sovereignty over the kingdom of mortals and gives it to whom he will" (Dan. 4:32). It is the hopeful "until" that debunks Nebuchadnezzar's hegemony and that exhibits it as a fragile penultimate power arrangement that cannot prevail. Nebuchadnezzar's big learning yet to come is that "Heaven is sovereign" (v. 26).

But then in verse 27, Daniel makes a move beyond interpretation. He dares to follow dream and interpretation with a policy proposal. This celebrated but uncredentialed Jew speaks Jewish truth to hegemonic power:

> Therefore, O king, may my counsel be acceptable to you; atone for your sins with righteousness, and your iniquities with mercy to the oppressed, so that your prosperity may be prolonged. (4:27)

Righteousness and mercy! Righteousness, which is to practice communitarian economics and ethics between haves and have-nots, and mercy, which is to yield to the neighbor in need. The outcome of these two practices is in order that "your prosperity may be prolonged." The calculus is simple: the practice of mercy will lead to prosperity. The calculus is as old as the book of Deuteronomy. But what is old and steady in Jewish horizon must have been a stunner to hegemonic power. It is a stunner because hegemonic power does not major in righteousness and does not specialize in mercy. Indeed, Daniel may have read Second Isaiah, in which Babylon is condemned for its treatment of Israel:

> I was angry with my people,
>   I profaned my heritage;
> I gave them into your hand,
>   you showed them no mercy;
> on the aged you made your yoke
>   exceedingly heavy.
>   Isa. 47:6

The proposal of Daniel to his overlord is that the crown may open its settled imperial truth to the countertruth that has been kept and nourished in this local tradition of Torah.

When Daniel finished speaking, the narrative tersely reports, "all this came upon Nebuchadnezzar" (Dan. 4:28). All this dream came upon him. All this dream of deconstruction and humiliation. All this dream came because Nebuchadnezzar had not grasped the Jewish "until," had not understood that his power was penultimate and held to account. All this came upon him, but none of it would have surprised any serious Jew. Nebuchadnezzar is presented as still being buoyantly full of himself:

> The king said, "Is this not magnificent Babylon, which I have built as a royal capital by my mighty power and for my glorious majesty?" (Dan. 4:30)

But, says the narrator, while the words were still in the king's mouth, a voice came from heaven:

> O King Nebuchadnezzar, to you it is declared: The kingdom has departed from you! (v. 31)

The drama of self-sufficiency is interrupted by another voice, this one the transcendent voice of heaven beyond the reach of the superpower. This interrupting voice is the same one that will sound again in the parable of the Rich Fool in Luke 12:

> God said to him, "You fool! This very night your life is being demanded of you. And the things you have prepared, whose will they be?" (Luke 12:20)

It is the big hovering question that is always asked of absolute power. That voice to Nebuchadnezzar lays out the dismantling and then reiterates "until you have learned that the Most High has sovereignty over the kingdom of mortals and gives it to whom he will" (Dan. 4:32).

The turn in the narrative occurs in verse 34, when Nebuchadnezzar himself attests, "My reason returned to me." He had been, he now acknowledges, unreasonable. Indeed, he had been insane. Absolute power, in its mix of anxiety and self-sufficiency, does indeed become insane. It becomes insane in acquisitiveness, in aggressive violence, in the seizure of goods that belong to others, in its craving disregard of local traditions. When reason returns to the dominant culture, it issues in doxology (vv. 34–35). This is not an idle "praise hymn," but a genuine acknowledgment and ceding over of authority. Nebuchadnezzar has finally, under the tutelage of Daniel, arrived at the inescapable "until" of penultimacy, where he never could have arrived himself without this Jewish witness. The narrative ends with restoration, on the other side of yielding:

> At that time my reason returned to me; and my majesty and splendor were restored to me for the glory of my kingdom. My counselors and my lords sought me out, I was re-established over my kingdom, and still more greatness was added to me. (Dan. 4:36)

But the reiteration is grounded in an acknowledgment:

> Now I, Nebuchadnezzar, praise and extol and honor the King of heaven,
>
>> for all his works are truth,
>>   and his ways are justice;
>> and he is able to bring low
>>   those who walk in pride.
>> 4:37

Truth and justice, not deception and exploitation. Not falseness and injustice. Nebuchadnezzar is sobered by his situation before the God of heaven.

III

That is as far as I will go now in the narrative of the hegemonic power of Nebuchadnezzar in the book of Daniel. Here are three narratives of confrontation in which an exemplary Jew responds out of his saving tradition for the sake of the world. I suggest these are three narrative pictures that pertain to our theme of hope restored, through biblical imagination, against empire, and for the sake of the world.

1. In chapter 2, Daniel, unlike the magicians of the empire, knows "the mysteries." He knows them for the sake of Nebuchadnezzar:

> But as for me, this mystery has not been revealed to me because of any wisdom that I have more than any other living being, but in order that the interpretation may be known to the king and that you may understand the thoughts of your mind. (Dan. 2:30)

It is important that this king should come to know, but he can know only by submitting to the truth entrusted to Daniel. There is a long tradition in biblical narrative of turning to this unlikely source:

- In Exodus 12:32, Pharaoh at long last comes to Moses and says, "And bring a blessing on me too."
- In Jeremiah 21:2, Zedekiah pleads with Jeremiah for the sake of Jerusalem:

  > Please inquire of the LORD on our behalf, for King Nebuchadrezzar of Babylon is making war against us; perhaps the LORD will perform a wonderful deed for us, as he has often done, and will make him withdraw from us.

- In John 18:38, the governor asks Jesus, "What is truth?"

In the biblical horizon, the world of power and control does not know the mystery that makes life possible. It is this mystery that has been entrusted to the unassimilated people of God.

In Christian confession, that mystery is this:

Christ has died.
Christ is risen.
Christ will come again.

In Jewish tradition, that mystery is that you cannot circumvent the requirement of righteousness and mercy. It is the same mystery. It is the truth that raw power and brutal control cannot generate the safety, well-being, or joy for which creaturely life is destined and in which it hopes. The church, as an heir to Daniel, has frittered most of its authority away on lesser matters. But here it is. It is the great "until" that Moses and Jeremiah and Jesus all know so well.

2. In chapter 3, Daniel and the three young Jews are so clear and so sure of their identity and destiny as the people of God that they refuse to bow down to the icons of hegemony. They refuse to credit, even for an instant, that the exhibition of power and glory by Nebuchadnezzar holds any gift for the future. Refusing to bow down is an act of bold defiance; Daniel and these courageous Jews refuse to entertain the thought that Nebuchadnezzar has in his power to make any claim on their life. This either-or defiance is, as we know, not the whole of Scripture. There are models of accommodation, not least in the Joseph narrative, which in some ways is a counterpoint to the Daniel narrative. Thus, the Daniel narrative may not be our last, best word on the matter. But it is a word that we may ponder for a season in order to ask how to recover nerve for the hope that has been entrusted to us, for without such recovered nerve we likely cannot act "for the sake of the world."

3. In chapter 4, it is clear that Daniel and the three young Jews' defiance in chapter 3 is not just stubbornness. It is, rather, stubbornness as a way of making distinctions and maintaining distance from which to articulate an alternative. It is clear that Daniel's defiance is "for the sake of the world," that is, for the sake of the empire. Daniel very much wants Nebuchadnezzar to embrace the "until." That is why in verse 27 he offers the double imperative of the road back to security. It is, in a proper theological sense, crazy to practice high-handed, aggressive, acquisitive ultimacy at the expense of the rule of the God of heaven. The news on the lips of the Jew is that there is an alternative to the lethal system of Nebuchadnezzar. There is a road back to well-being and even back to authority. It is a conversion from exploitation to righteousness. It is a transformation from arrogance to mercy.

The news is that there is an alternative to the mad pursuit of commodity; it is the maintenance of the neighbor. There is an alternative to aggressive consumerism; it is the sharing of resources. There is an alternative to imperial militarism; it is to yield ultimacy in the interest of a peaceable order. The issue is articulated in the narrative as addressed to high worldly power. But the same news is offered to every person who is bewitched by the ideology of autonomy that lies just beneath the surface of conservative starchiness and liberal accommodation.

So imagine this Daniel,

- entrusted with the life to which Nebuchadnezzar has no claim;
- empowered in boldness to defiance for the sake of an alternative destiny;
- knowledgeable about the conversion whereby the world may come to well-being;
- knowledgeable as a practical theologian.

He is indeed a person of hope and faith for the sake of the world.

Questions for Reflection

1. Identity is a central concern throughout the book of Daniel, as its Jewish protagonists live in a society of pluralism and possible idolatry. In today's pluralist world, how is your identity shaped by your faith? How does your identity as a person of faith lead you to transformative actions?

2. Righteousness and mercy are the antithesis of hegemonic power as shown in Daniel's interpretation of Nebuchadnezzar's dream. What are some examples of how righteousness and mercy have challenged and even transformed empires of power? What role have truth and justice played in these examples?

3. Daniel 3 features three young Jews who boldly resist their king by refusing to bow down to him in great defiance. In what ways can your identity as a person of faith and hope lead you to protest boldly?

4. Daniel was a practical theologian who articulated, embodied, and acted out theological claims in the public sphere. As you journey in this study, can you view yourself like Daniel? How does this look in your life? How do you help others be practical theologians as Daniel did?

Chapter 8

Hope in God's Future, Grounded in Holiness

(Daniel 1; 7–12)

I

The previous chapter saw that Daniel is a character of hope and faith entrusted, empowered, and knowledgeable, who has an immense impact upon the world because of his faith. The narrative is surely intended as a model to Jews of faith about life in the world. Such models of courageous faith, moreover, are offered as a model for Christian courage:

> And what more should I say? For time would fail me to tell of Gideon, Barak, Samson, Jephthah, of David and Samuel and the prophets—who through faith conquered kingdoms, administered justice, obtained promises, shut the mouths of lions, quenched raging fire, escaped the edge of the sword, won strength out of weakness, became mighty in war, put foreign armies to flight. (Heb. 11:32–34)

To be sure, in that list the models come from an earlier period and Daniel is not named. But the phrases fit Daniel as well: "administered justice, obtained promises, shut the mouths of lions, quenched raging fire." My question now is this: How did Daniel become equipped for such a life of courageous hope? For that matter, how did any of those named in the recital of Hebrews 11 become so equipped? While most of us have no inclination for such heroism, we might learn from them how to be better equipped for such risk. The question is, How did Daniel come to this calling?

I propose that the answer to the question is offered in Daniel 1, even though I am aware that the narratives have only incidental connection to each other. Perhaps there is a reason that chapter 1 comes in the book before chapters 2–4. In chapter 1, we learn of the reach of the empire into the Jewish community to equip suitable Jewish agents for civil service in the empire. To seek such Jews who are handsome, without physical defect, knowledgeable, insightful, and competent makes sense to me. It is rather like a government "out East" seeking good Midwesterners because they are reliable, or corporate executives preferring upper Midwestern Lutherans because people from Lake Wobegon are without guile and trustworthy. They knew that about Jews in the empire, and so they recruited young Jews for their imperial training program in service to the empire. The ones selected had to leave their Jewish families to enter the training program. To help them move from their Jewish rootage to the horizon of the empire, they received imperial names; Belteshazzar used to be Daniel, and Shadrach, Meshach, and Abednego are known in the narrative primarily by their imperial names, not their old Jewish names of Hananiah, Mishael, and Azariah. Perhaps even our reading of them is already saturated in the reality of hegemony.

The pivot point of the training program and of the narrative is the training table at the imperial boot camp:

> The king assigned them a daily portion of the royal rations of food and wine. They were to be educated for three years, so that at the end of that time they could be stationed in the king's court. (Dan. 1:5)

But get this:

> But Daniel resolved that he would not defile himself with the royal rations of food and wine; so he asked the palace master to allow him not to defile himself. (1:8)

"Resolved"—set it upon his heart. Daniel refused the diet of the training table, an act that ordinarily would have gotten him dismissed from the program. It might be like training for an accounting firm but insisting that your work will be done on an abacus. From his loyalty to Jewish identity, Daniel concluded that such alien imperial food would defile him and render him a disqualified Jew.

He asked the palace master, the director of recruits, to be given permission to eat other food. The palace master was not unsympathetic to Daniel but declared that if he gave permission and Daniel was seen to be unhealthy in any way, it would be his head. Interestingly, the narrative does not report what the palace master decided, but apparently he said to this stubborn Jew, "You work it out with your guard, but don't tell me about it." So Daniel's business is now with the guard who has charge over Daniel, Shadrach, Meshach, and Abednego. It is telling that midway through the narrative, the four are called by their Jewish names and not their new imperial names. The narrator trusts his implied audience to notice: still Jews!

Because of the proposal to depart from the official rules of engagement at the training table, the guard agrees to extend the experiment. Ten days of Jewish vegetables and Jewish water contrasted with the rich royal rations. At the end of the ten-day experiment, the guard saw that the Jewish boys were "better and fatter" than all the others in the program. As a result, the guard, and perhaps the palace master as well, though he is not mentioned here, judged that there was no risk for them in the alternative, no risk for their jobs or for their lives. The Jewish proposal was free of such risk. Consequently, the guard permitted the four Jews an alternative for the three-year training program. No royal rations for them. And then, we are told,

> To these four young men God gave knowledge and skill in every aspect of literature and wisdom; Daniel also had insight into all visions and dreams. (1:17)

It worked! They are still Jews!

At the end of the three-year program, at the graduation ceremony, Nebuchadnezzar came for the awarding of prizes and diplomas and did not find other recruits to compare with the blessed four:

> In every matter of wisdom and understanding concerning which the king inquired of them, he found them ten times better than all the magicians and enchanters in his whole kingdom. (1:20)

Imagine that—ten times better! The narrative carries us stage by stage so that you can see the tension thicken:

the recruitment
the offer and the refusal

the palace master
the guard and the ten-day experiment
the three-year training session
the verdict: ten times better

Voila! Daniel is qualified and commended for service to the empire, but he has not compromised his Jewishness. It is his identity in faith that gives him a hope-filled way to be in the world for the sake of the world.

Here is my thesis. It is Daniel's refusal to be "defiled" that gives him the power, the courage, and the authority in chapters 2, 3, and 4 to make a difference in the empire. So I dwell on the term "defile." The term used twice here is, in the Old Testament, found only in the following literature:

- In Zephaniah 3:1, the term is juxtaposed to oppression and autonomy; the defiled city "accepted no correction."
- In Lamentations 4:14, the city is defiled with blood, that is, murder.
- In Isaiah 59:3, it is defiled by blood (murder), iniquity, and lies.
- In Isaiah 63:3, it is "stained" by blood.
- In Malachi 1:7, 12, it is defiled by polluted offerings and profanation of the Lord's table.
- In Ezra 2:62 it is defiled by impure genealogy for priests, so also in Nehemiah 7:64.

That is the sum of all the uses of the term. The various occurrences of the term cluster around ritual and social activity that violate Torah and compromise Jewish identity. A strong tilt of the term is toward ritual contamination, though the references to murder are social rather than ritual. But if we take the term in context, according to this word usage, Daniel refused to engage in a diet that would violate his purity, thus offering a usage related to a ritual disqualification.

Now I am aware that many of us are wary of the holiness traditions, most especially those of us whose theological tradition focuses upon grace without these punctilious requirements. But I believe that the Daniel text and the holiness tradition may have a good word for us if we focus on the main point and are not distracted by the specificity of the requirements about which it is easy to take exception.

If we consider defilement and pollution as a compromise of faithful identity, then holiness requires a distancing from the compromises offered by culture that erode identity, that subvert courageous hope, and that ease resolve into accommodation.

In most mainline Protestant churches in the United States, the deep problem for responding to the gospel is not excessive punctiliousness, though it may be in some quarters. Rather, the crisis is one of easy cultural accommodation so that the sharp edge of discipline is nearly lost—any form of discipleship being too readily slotted in legalism and moralism and narrowness. If the danger to the church's testimony is the loss of missional passion for responding to the gospel, then I think that we have something to learn from the Daniel traditions.

Another Daniel, Daniel Smith-Christopher, has suggested that the practice of purity is a mode of hope-filled resistance to empire in that ancient Jewish tradition.[1] Daniel's attention to dietary practice is not because he is a legalist, but because he is ready to engage in resistance against imperial hegemony, for which Nebuchadnezzar is the cipher in the narrative. Daniel's dietary refusal is as much an act of defiance as the later refusal to bow down in chapter 3, even if the refusal to bow down is more dramatic and a compromise on food would have been no big deal. What Daniel does in this narrative is to refuse the junk food of the empire that would render him compromised and without standing ground in his identity. He refuses junk food and instead settles for Jewish health food (vegetables and water), which not only nourishes his body in strength but also nourishes his faith identity in hopeful resolve. Thus, against the teaching of Mark 7:15, sometimes what goes in may indeed defile, if defilement means the compromise of faith identity.

II

Thus I propose—with perhaps too many doubtful interpretive nuances—that we may learn from the Daniel narrative that the capacity for faithful response to the gospel for the hope of the world begins in a disciplined practice of holiness that refuses junk food that compromises an evangelical identity. The empire always wants the faithful community to believe that its junk food is at least harmless and, at best, good for you.

At the first level such junk food is indeed "junk food," the offer of artificial foods that contain nothing of what is needed for health.[2] The politicization of the Centers for Disease Control in Atlanta is an indication of how much the food and drug industry wants to distort habits of usage in the interest of making money.

But at a second level, the real junk food that is offered by dominant ideology is the ideology of insecurity and anxiety that convinces us to hope that more commodities—more sex or beer or oil—can contribute to health and well-being and youth.

That commoditization of human possibility is fostered by the wonders of electronic liturgy: cell phones, email, Facebook, Twitter, Instagram, and all the existing models of communication that lead to dumbing down and fake community. One does not need to be a Luddite—and I am not one—to see that the offers of a virtual society are a feeble substitute for serious human engagement that requires critical thought and genuine care. I do not want to defend all the rules and regulations of Leviticus and all the attempts to regulate holiness into a sacerdotal system. And I do not want to applaud Daniel's resistance to the empire if it is to be understood as a thin moralism that simply wants to honor a code. But I believe that Daniel's resistance is not a regimented sacerdotal system or thin moralism. It is, rather, a knowing, intentional act of self-consciousness that a distinction must be made between the risky offers of Nebuchadnezzar and the realities of faith. That discipline did not cause Daniel to withdraw from Nebuchadnezzar's system of civil service. Indeed, verse 21 attests that Daniel continued in the service of Nebuchadnezzar until the first year of Cyrus the Persian.

Daniel was able to make a distinction that is grounded in the decree of Exodus 9 concerning the pestilence that will come upon Egypt:

> But the LORD will make a distinction between the livestock of Israel and the livestock of Egypt, so that nothing shall die of all that belongs to the Israelites. . . . And on the next day the LORD did so; all the livestock of the Egyptians died, but of the livestock of the Israelites not one died. (Exod. 9:4, 6)

That distinction is mostly lost among us. And the outcome, I suggest, is at best an anemic capacity to respond to the gospel for the hope of the world.

So consider Daniel as a man undefiled, unseduced by empire, uncompromised in faith. He is just a model and not more. I understand that none of us and none of our parishioners are ready for that kind of heroic distinction, because it smacks too much of self-righteousness self-justification. But it would not hurt to raise the question about what kind of food the empire offers:

> Do not work for the food that perishes, but for the food that endures for eternal life, which the Son of Man will give you. For it is on him that God the Father has set his seal.[3] (John 6:27)

Or what kind of water gives life:

> Jesus said to her, "Everyone who drinks of this water will be thirsty again, but those who drink of the water that I will give them will never be thirsty. The water that I will give will become in them a spring of water gushing up to eternal life." (4:13–14)

It is no wonder that the crowd said of his bread, "Sir, give us this bread always" (John 6:34). And on that occasion the woman said of the water, "Sir, give me this water, so that I may never be thirsty or have to keep coming here to draw water" (4:15). Thus, undefiled Daniel had no appetite for the junk food of Nebuchadnezzar.

- It is this Daniel who in chapter 2 knew the mystery that would let the empire receive true teaching about its future.
- It was Daniel's friend who in chapter 3 refused to bow down and in the end evoked a doxology for his God on the lips of the empire.
- It is this Daniel who in chapter 4 could instruct the king in the ways of righteousness and mercy, who permitted the empire to cover its sanctity by yielding its ultimacy to the God of heaven.

I am not sure that chapter 1 is the trigger in the book of Daniel for chapters 2, 3, and 4, but I suspect so. One last thought on this connection: After the vision in Acts 10 of eating what used to be unclean, the meeting in Acts 15 reached a conclusion that included the verdict of James:

> Therefore I have reached the decision that we should not trouble those Gentiles who are turning to God, but we should write to them to abstain only from things polluted by idols and from fornication and from whatever has been strangled and from blood. (Acts 15:19–20)

Do not "trouble." The early church was invited to watch out for food polluted by idols:

> For it has seemed good to the Holy Spirit and to us to impose on you no further burden than these essentials: that you abstain from what has been sacrificed to idols and from blood and from what is strangled and from fornication. If you keep yourselves from these, you will do well. Farewell. (15:28–29)

If this analysis is credible and the avoidance of defilement was urgent for the courage of faith amid the empire, then the pastoral teaching in the church must do the hard imaginative work of identifying food that defiles. The intent is not a community preoccupied with excessive disciplines. It is, rather, a community clear enough in its identity that it can bear witness precisely to and hope in the truth entrusted to it. What better than holy disciplines, whereby we, with Nebuchadnezzar, may recover the sanity of faith and sing songs of praise:

> [F]or all his works are truth,
> and his ways are justice;
> and he is able to bring low
> those who walk in pride.
> Dan. 4:37

III

The second half of the book of Daniel is of a completely different genre, offering *visions* that bespeak an apocalyptic horizon (chaps. 7–12). Indeed, these chapters are the primary representative (along with Zech. 9–14) of apocalyptic literature in the Hebrew Bible, the visionary dimension of faith that was so crucial in the emergence of the Christian movement. The visions gather together historical memories and present awarenesses into a massive act of theological imagination whereby present time, present circumstance, and present generation are identified as a break point in human history. In that break point, the raw sovereignty of God impinges decisively and even violently upon human history, in order to overwhelm all competing powers, and in order to create a new world as a hospitable place where the small community of the faithful will prosper and be safe. The accent is upon the inbreaking of divine power that no longer pays any attention to the political realities featured in the earlier narratives; unimpeded by such realities, the inbreaking causes the decisive end of what was and, by implication, generates an entirely new beginning of a new world for the faithful. That characteristic apocalyptic articulation, sketched out by a number of scholars, is utilized in Daniel 7–12 for a quite particular purpose, namely, to comment upon and interpret the crisis of 167–164 BCE that so threatened Jews and Jewishness.[4] Thus apocalyptic rhetoric is here linked to a particular historical reality, so that apocalyptic hope is not in a vacuum, but concerns real people in real circumstances.

The traditioning process that combined the earlier narratives of chapters 1–6 and the later visions of chapters 7–12 is more complex than we are able to explain. Yet the combination of narratives and visions together forms something of a coherent theological statement, though, as elsewhere in the Old Testament, the new coherence does not overrun all the earlier textual particularities. Nonetheless, it is clear that both narratives and visions (in both Aramaic and Hebrew) attest to a single theological claim, namely, that the God of Israel is the defining agent in human history and in world history, an agent in which the Jews can fully trust and before whom the Gentiles finally must yield.

Thus the sum of the theological claim is a great assertion of hope that empowers responding Jews to great acts of courageous obedience in the face of alien powers that grow even more alien and ominous as we move from narrative to vision. However odd the imagining offered here and however difficult the critical questions, the focus is upon the same hope that is given us in these several genres, hope that matters in the real world of hostile power, hope that is situated beyond historical processes in the holy mystery of God, who presides over heaven and earth but who has disclosed the time of ending and beginning only to God's beloved people. Thus the process of hope for Jews is to let Jews know about the divine intention for the future that remains completely hidden from obtuse Gentiles, who trouble and posture but who finally face harsh judgment and ultimate failure.

In the vision section of the book, I note four particularly important texts.

1. In 7:13–14 a poetic interpretation of the "coming one" is voiced that has been immensely important in subsequent interpretation. The "Ancient of Days" (so RSV; rendered in NRSV as the "Ancient One") refers to the high, transcendent God. But interpretive interest has focused rather upon the phrase "a son of man" (so RSV; rendered in NRSV as "a human being"). The juxtaposition of these two figures—"Ancient of Days" and "son of man"—is a promise that the high transcendent God, whose sovereignty is completely sure, will have dominion and kingship established in the earth through an agent, the "son of man." Interpretation, however, has struggled with the intention of and identification of the "son of man."

Two issues are important. First, W. Sibley Towner has helpfully explored the issue of whether "coming with the clouds" means a descent of a heavenly being in a theophany or an ascent of a human agent in an apotheosis; he argues for the latter, that the coming one is a human agent, "a figure for a fifth human monarchy."[5] But if human, then the second question is whether this royal figure is an individual and thus a king, or whether the phrase refers to the entire kingdom as a collective entity. Towner opts for the latter, concluding that it represents the Jewish community of the time as persecuted by the Syrian king.[6] Such an interpretation indicates the quite direct way in which this promise for the future is made to a particular group of Jews with the urging that they should remain obedient, faithful, and trusting in the midst of adversity. It is likely that this particular group of the pious is to be contrasted with the militant Zealots of the Maccabean movement, who sought to establish an earthly kingdom of their own. Here the imagery and the expectation are wholly on being *receptive* to the new order that God would give.

Towner's reading is cogent, but we are dealing with highly metaphorical, poetic phrases that are rooted in older mythic traditions, so that the meanings are not clear and likely are not stable. The history of interpretation has been open to rich alternative readings in various contexts, as Towner's own commentary makes clear. It is important for Christian readers to recognize how this particular text in 7:13–14 was taken up in the earliest Christian proclamation that was rooted in apocalyptic horizons.[7] It is clear that in order to proclaim (a) the coming of God's new regime, and (b) Jesus as the bringer of that new regime, the attestation of the early church utilized the Daniel traditions that were mythically rooted but, as in the book of Daniel, linked to a quite historical moment, in this case the moment of Jesus through whom the kingdom is "at hand" (Mark 1:14–15; see esp. Mark 13:14–27 for a primal Christian use of the tradition).

2. Whereas 7:13–14 links together "son of man" and the "Ancient of Days" who will enact the new kingdom, 7:18, 21, and 25 speak of "the holy ones of the Most High" who "shall receive the kingdom and possess the kingdom forever—forever and ever" (Dan. 7:18). The identity of this community has been the subject of important critical reflection. There is no doubt that this visionary material is rooted in a mythic tradition that imagined God in the heavenly court surrounded by legions of angels who attend to the heavenly king.[8] Out of that appeal to a much older mythic, liturgical tradition, Martin Noth has argued that the "holy ones" were originally divine beings, "heavenly associates of God."[9] The tradition, however, has transposed this phrasing so that it now refers to the human community of the faithful who adhere in obedience to the "Most High," and who shall receive the new rule of God.

Thus the tradition has taken old mythic imagery about heavenly matters and has connected them to a historical crisis. Taken together then, "son of man" and "holy ones" now concern the community that has acted defiantly against established powers and according to the will of the "Ancient of Days." This cluster of images, given through these visionary texts, concerns a new community of the faithful who live in hope. While they hope, they act in radical obedience, in order to receive what the Most High God will give, namely, a new world of well-being.

3. Special attention should be given to the prayer offered in Daniel 9:4–19. This prayer (which has particular resonance with long prayers also set in the Persian period in Ezra 9 and Neh. 9) is odd in

context. It does, however, focus on two particular matters: (a) Israel's petitions for and dependence upon God's forgiveness in a circumstance of persecution, where compromise and accommodation must have been powerful seductions, and (b) the reliability of God as a keeper of covenant. Thus the prayer may be understood as an actual transaction between God and Israel. It is also, however, an important piece of theological affirmation that serves as a grounding of hope, rooted in the conviction that God is "a keeper of covenant."[10]

4. Daniel 12:1–3 is one of two texts in the Old Testament that clearly attest to the resurrection of the dead (the other is Isa. 26:19, but see also Isa. 25:6–10a). In Daniel 12:1–3 a double resurrection is anticipated, some to everlasting life and some to everlasting shame and contempt. (The vision of that twofold judgment is replicated in the parable of Matt. 25:31–46.) Beyond the joyous promise of Isaiah 26:19, which speaks of resurrection only in terms of joy, this text in the book of Daniel contemplates both joy and judgment beyond death. It is clear that this affirmation of life beyond death, which is only at the fringes of the Old Testament, is able to speak of resurrection as a function of *the end* (12:13) that is also the *beginning* of *new life*. That is, resurrection is a vehicle for radical apocalyptic thought that bespeaks fearful endings and amazing beginnings, all of which are wrought by the power of God.

It is clear that the resurrection in early Christian preaching was also a function of a world-ending and world-beginning proclamation. It is an immense loss for the church that this deep understanding has been largely trivialized and privatized so that the resurrection is timidly taken to be resuscitation or restoration to one's loved ones, either notion of which minimizes the large hope claimed in God's sovereignty, a sovereignty that at the end will judge and save.

IV

Apocalyptic is a rhetorical strategy for articulating deep hope that lies beyond the vagaries of historical reality. This is not a world-escaping hope; rather, it is a summons to obedience that refuses accommodation to the rulers of the old age. Thus the narrative is witness to the rule of God, who sustains the practitioners of truth in the presence of power, and the visions intensify the claim for God's rule that is so powerful, so majestic, and so mysterious that none can resist. This rhetoric of hope in the resurrection links the most sweeping mystery of God to the most concrete practice of a name-able community. That connection amounts in poetic imagery and in disciplined practice to a dismissive disregard of the rulers of this age, who will be terminated at "the end." The book of Daniel represents a daring and outrageous invitation to hope in a God who is not ordered or domesticated or generated by historical facts on the ground. This text invites believers to wager everything on that which is not in hand but surely promised.

In the Hebrew ordering of the canon, the book of Daniel is placed after Esther, and just before the cluster of materials in Ezra, Nehemiah, and Chronicles. That is, the book of Daniel is situated in the midst of the Persian literature, suggesting that Jewishness-amid-empire is the characteristic context for Jews at the end of the Hebrew canon. It is the challenge for Jews in a Persian milieu—or extrapolated into the Hellenistic environment of Antiochus— to see if Jewishness can yield futures in and through and beyond the capacity of the empire. In some instances the book of Daniel sees the hegemony of the empire in the person of Nebuchadnezzar as a way to the future. More often it sees God's newness in spite of the empire, which must end. Either way, hope is linked to lived reality, for God's newness will be given in a world of power where truth may be fragile but endlessly insistent. Clearly the process of canon did not intend to keep this material tied to the Persian context. In the dynamism of the tradition, the text moves beyond Persian realities to the defining Jewish reality of trusting in a future-generating God.

In the ordering of the Christian Bible, the book of Daniel is resituated among the Prophets. This alternative canonical location accents the point that the book of Daniel anticipates God's new future and so is congruent with the great literature of prophetic hope. It is surely the case that the hope given in the book of Daniel is offered in a different genre of narrative and vision and thus in important ways differs from the most characteristic prophetic genres. The accent on the future, however, is enough to assert, now in a prophetic context, the newness of the God who cannot be resisted and who invites a trusting obedience in the present for the soon-to-come newness of

God's future. It is on the basis of such future that the church end-lessly prays, "Thine is the kingdom and the power and the glory."

In such a prayer of anticipation, the church evokes the phrasing of Daniel 7:14:

> To him was given dominion
>   and glory and kingship,
> that all peoples, nations, and languages
>   should serve him.
> His dominion is an everlasting dominion
>   that shall not pass away,
> and his kingship is one
>   that shall never be destroyed.

The surging of apocalyptic cadence, moreover, does not stop until that future is voiced doxologically:

> Then the seventh angel blew his trumpet, and there were loud voices in heaven, saying,
>   "The kingdom of the world has become the kingdom of our
>   Lord
>   and of his Messiah,
>   and he will reign forever and ever."
>   Rev. 11:15

The singing church waits. It waits confidently. And while wait-ing, it obeys in confidence, unimpressed by the alternative obedience always imposed by the "little horn" of the empires (see Dan. 7:8) and often resisted by a "little help" from one's comrades (see Dan. 11:34). In the end, neither the "little horn" that resists nor the "little help" that assists matters much, because, finally, it is God alone who gives futures according to this subversive tradition.

Questions for Reflection

1. Daniel and his companions carried their identity as Jewish people with them as they gained knowledge and served the empire. Through this preservation of identity, they were able to remain faithful to God. What is your core identity? And how might that identity be used to serve others or to dismantle empires of oppression?

2. Brueggemann states that defilement is going against or compromising identity. In Daniel's case, maintaining identity meant sticking to a diet that was based around ritual and his Jewishness. What are the things in your life that may defile your identity? What are the systems in our world that may try to push you away from your authenticity?

3. The empire can be a seducing agent with empty promises derived from capitalism and other systems that harm ourselves and others. This "junk food" offered by the empire is tempting. What kind of junk food is the empire offering you right now? How have you participated in this junk food feast?

4. Daniel invites us to follow and hope in a God who goes beyond orderliness, domestication, or historical conditions. Often we want order, so that we may feel comfortable, but it seems the God of Daniel and other biblical narratives cannot be contained. What thoughts and feelings arise in you as you ponder our uncontainable and mysterious God?

Chapter 9

The Nagging Hope of the Lament Psalms

Exegetical and Homiletical Focus

Exegetical Focus: Truth-Telling as Well-Making

The lament psalms in the book of Psalms voice a clear, thick, deep, shrewd understanding of the processes that are indispensable for the transformation of the "human condition" from death to life, from sorrow to joy, from anger to energy, from despair to hope. (A fresh understanding of these indispensable processes, so utterly Jewish, was reasserted in the modern world by Sigmund Freud.) These lament psalms offer rich variation in particulars. But the general flow of rhetoric that performs these indispensable processes is clear enough to trace, as scholarship has done, as a reliable, persistent pattern that amounts to a describable genre. This genre of speech features a human speaker who is filled with sufficient chutzpah to voice truth in honest ways before the Lord of the covenant. That recurring rhetoric is grounded in the conviction that God's covenant partners have entitlement in the covenant to address God. More than that, these entitled speakers seize the initiative in such speech and dare to summon God into their vexation that is the subject of such lament, protest, and complaint. They assume authority to state their case before God with hope-filled expectations that God is willing, able, and ready to engage with them in the vexation.

I

This recurring pattern of speech features the covenantal partner drawing God into trouble with a hopeful expectation that if God can be mobilized, the trouble can be assuaged! I may readily identify three features in this patterned speech. First, the psalmist regularly *addresses God by name*: "LORD (YHWH)." The utterance of the holy name affirms that the speaker is intimately and confidently connected to the God who is addressed—thus, "My God, my God" (Ps. 22:1); "O LORD" (3:1); "O God of my right" (4:1); "O LORD my God" (7:1).

Second, the speaker voices a specific *complaint*, describing for God the particulars of trouble, often an attack by enemies, being shamed and slandered, being abandoned, being sick, being vulnerable, or being weak:

> O LORD, how many are my foes!
>   Many are rising against me.
>   Ps. 3:1

> I am distraught by the noise of the enemy,
>   because of the clamor of the wicked.
> For they bring trouble upon me,
>   and in anger they cherish enmity against me.
>   55:2–3

> . . . [P]eople trample on me;
>   all day long foes oppress me;
> my enemies trample on me all day long,
>   for many fight against me.
>   56:1–2

> I lie down among lions
>   that greedily devour human prey;
> their teeth are spears and arrows,
>   their tongues sharp swords.
>   57:4

The descriptions are vivid and specific; they are, at the same time, open and imaginative enough that in our use of these psalms we may fill them with imagery from our own experience.

The third feature is that when the complaint has been sufficiently detailed to move God, it is accompanied by vigorous *imperatives* that ask God to rectify circumstances that are unmerited and unbearable and before which the speaker is helpless:

Rise up, O LORD!
Deliver me, O my God!
3:7

Answer me when I call, O God of my right! . . .
Be gracious to me, and hear my prayer.
4:1

Be gracious to me, O LORD, for I am languishing;
O LORD, heal me, for my bones are shaking with terror.
6:2

Rise up, O LORD, in your anger;
lift yourself up against the fury of my enemies;
awake, O my God.
7:6

O God, break the teeth in their mouths;
tear out the fangs of the young lions, O LORD!
58:6

These imperatives are unrestrained in their vigor, in their emotional force, and even in their violence. These are acts of urgency that, insofar as they are imperatives, issue commands to God, in the hopeful expectation that this covenant partner will be attentive and responsive.

These three elements together amount to framing the God relationship around the needs of the speaker—in contrast to doxologies, in which all the attention is given over to God. Thus, provisionally, in the lament psalms the speaker assumes the dominant and primary role in the relationship and is able to take a daring and necessary initiative.

II

Two recurring elements in this patterned speech constitute difficulty for those who want pastoral care (and Christian piety in general) to be "nice." First, the lament psalms are permeated with *motivations* that give God reason to be attentive and to act. It is as though when God hears the unrestrained imperatives, God responds, "Now why should I bother to answer your demand?" Such motivations may seem ignoble to us, because they sound like bargaining that ought not to happen with God. They are, however, efforts to make clear to God that God has something at stake in the vexation of the speaker and should act for God's self-interest. Or as we say, "For your name's sake," that is, for the sake of your reputation. God should act on behalf of the speaker and so be on exhibit as a trustworthy God. This act will maintain and enhance God's reputation (about which God is thought to care!) as a faithful covenant partner. Thus, for example, the speaker may remind God of God's previous fidelity as the basis for their hope that it ought now be continued in the present circumstance:

> In you our ancestors trusted;
>> they trusted, and you delivered them.
> To you they cried, and were saved;
>> in you they trusted and were not put to shame.
>>>> 22:4–5

Most daringly, the psalmist warns God that if the speaker dies, there will be one less voice to praise God. This is on the assumption that God relishes praise and enjoys it:

> What profit is there in my death,
>> if I go down to the Pit?
> Will the dust praise you?
>> Will it tell of your faithfulness?
>>>> 30:9

> Do the shades rise up to praise you?
> Is your steadfast love declared in the grave,
>> or your faithfulness in Abaddon?
> Are your wonders known in the darkness,
>> or your saving help in the land of forgetfulness?
>>>> 88:10–12

The hope is that God will act for the speaker in God's own self-interest. In dire straits it is not a surprise that the petitioner will engage in regressive speech!

The other "objectionable" element in the laments is what scholars term *imprecation,* that is, a wish for vengeance on one's enemies. Most notoriously, in Psalm 109 the speaker inveighs against the enemy at length:

May his days be few;
   may another seize his position.
May his children be orphans,
   and his wife a widow.
May his children wander about and beg;
   may they be driven out of the ruins they inhabit.
May the creditor seize all that he has;
   may strangers plunder the fruits of his toil.
May there be no one to do him a kindness,
   nor anyone to pity his orphaned children.
May his posterity be cut off,
   may his name be blotted out in the second generation.
                                                      109:8–13

Break the arm of the wicked and evildoers;
   seek out their wickedness until you find none.
                                                      10:15

Let them vanish like water that runs away;
   like grass let them be trodden down and wither.
Let them be like the snail that dissolves into slime;
   like the untimely birth that never sees the sun.
                                                      58:7–8

Some of the pious will think that the faithful should not talk this way, and certainly not in the presence of the Holy One. Behind that is the notion that the faithful should not think that way or feel that way. But we do! Israel knew from the outset that what is felt and thought must be said; it must be said out loud, and it must be said out loud in the presence of God. This is the God from whom no secret can be hid![1] Truth-telling through such laments is completely without restraint or reservation, because it is truth-telling to the very bottom of the life of the speaker. Of course, the speaker does not herself act out these violent wishes for vengeance but only voices them to God, in whom the speaker has complete confidence.

When we consider these five elements together—address to God, complaint, petition, motivation, and imprecation—we are able to see that this is honest speech in the process of truth-telling. It is an act whereby the self, diminished by many "toils and snares," is now reclaimed and restored in the presence of God. The utterance amounts to a moment of "omnipotence" and audacious hope for the speaker, in which she dares presume that her cause deserves and will receive the full attention of the Holy God.[2]

This moment of utterance is an instance of *being heard*, that is, being heard back to full personhood. Thus, the opening imperative of such speech is often "Listen to me!":

> Answer me. (4:1)
> Give ear, . . . give heed. (5:1)
> Hear, O Lord! (30:10)
> Hear my prayer. (54:2)
> Give ear to my prayer. . . . Attend to me, and answer me. (55:1–2)

Self-announcement is the first step in the recovery of a self that has been depleted. But self-announcement counts only if it is addressed to someone in whom there is hope and confidence of being taken with utmost seriousness. Utmost seriousness on the part of God grounds this daring, unrestrained speech of the self who is ready to risk full exposure.

III

At this point in this patterned speech there is often a turn in rhetoric or at least a pause. One can see this in the abrupt newness of Psalms 13:5–6 and 22:21b, in which there is inexplicable resolution for the speaker. It is as though the speaker has spent his energy and has no more to say. Or perhaps the speaker pauses in the hope of receiving a response from the one addressed. The outcome of such speech is not automatic or guaranteed. It is a leap to the faithfulness of God that God enacts in freedom. It is risky speech, given fidelity-in-freedom on God's side, but these prayers characteristically end in a good, hopeful resolve of being heard by God:

> [T]he Lord has heard the sound of my weeping.
> The Lord has heard my supplication;
>   the Lord accepts my prayer.
>   6:8–9

In my distress I called upon the LORD;
    to my God I called.
From his temple he heard my voice,
    and my cry to him reached his ears.
                                    2 Sam. 22:7

But you heard my supplications
    when I cried out to you for help.
                                    Ps. 31:22b

This poor soul cried, and was heard by the LORD,
    and was saved from every trouble.
                                    34:6

I waited patiently for the LORD;
    he inclined to me and heard my cry.
                                    40:1

I love the LORD, because he has heard
    my voice and my supplications.
Because he inclined his ear to me,
    therefore I will call on him as long as I live.
                                    116:1–2

Being heard when engaged in truth-telling is a moment of verification, recognition, valorization, being taken seriously. It is an act
of emancipation. This is indeed truth-telling that makes free and that
makes well. Such a prayer characteristically ends in joyous thanksgiving, perhaps expressed in a thank offering:

What shall I return to the LORD
    for all his bounty to me?
I will lift up the cup of salvation
    and call on the name of the LORD.
I will pay my vows to the LORD
    in the presence of all his people.
                                    116:12–14

Or it may issue in glad testimony to the community:

> I have told the glad news of deliverance
>   in the great congregation;
> see, I have not restrained my lips.
>
> 40:9

Or endless doxology into future generations:

> From you comes my praise in the great congregation;
>   my vows I will pay before those who fear him. . . .
> Posterity will serve him;
>   future generations will be told about the Lord.
>
> 22:25, 30

In a variety of forms, these laments culminate in gladness, well-being, and readiness for a new life fully in sync with the faithful God who has restored. The truth that makes free and that makes well is a part of the process of *the reconstitution of the self* that has been depleted by a variety of assaults.

Of course, we must reckon with the occurrences of this patterned speech when it does not eventuate in such good resolve. This is evident in the individual laments of Psalms 39 and 88 and in the communal lament of Psalm 44. These psalms serve as reminders that in the free interaction of covenant partners, there are no guarantees. The entire interaction is risky. That same risk, of course, is present in every serious relationship of honest truth-telling.

IV

How odd it is that these rich resources of the community of faith that occupy so much of the book of Psalms have been almost completely lost in the life of the church, being absent (except for Psalm 22) in the liturgical sequence of the church.[3] Such an absence from the liturgy is in the interest of a polite spirituality that thinks that such abrasive truth-telling has no proper place in the life of the congregation. Such an absence in the practice of the church is an invitation to denial, the bet that such truth-telling is inappropriate before the God of all truth, and thus amounts to an undermining of hope.

The church has devised two strategies for embarrassed silencing of these texts and their best practice. The positive strategy is the

Midrashic Moment: Psalm 22 and Jesus

The opening line of Psalm 22 will be familiar to many Christian readers as the words Jesus cries out from the cross: "My God, my God, why have you forsaken me?" (Mark 15:34; Matt. 27:46). Although Jesus is presented as uttering only the first line of this psalm of lament, clearly the reader of the Gospel is supposed to recall the psalm as a whole, as the author works in several other references to it, including the dividing of the garments (Ps. 22:18), the piercing of hands and feet (22:16), and the mocking of passersby (22:7–8). The idea of Jesus being "forsaken" by God is of course a powerfully tragic effect of using Psalm 22 in the passion scene. At the same time, we are surely to note that the lament of Psalm 22 eventually turns toward salvation and praise (vv. 22–31), thus presaging Jesus' eventual resurrection. Indeed, the gospel story as a whole mirrors the basic psalmic pattern of *orientation* (Jesus' initial ministry), *disorientation* (the passion and death), and *new orientation* (the resurrection). As both the psalmist and the Gospel writer affirm, however, the new orientation can be had only by traveling through the disorientation. There is no shortcut through the pain.

development of pastoral care and particularly (at least in the United States) the "pastoral care movement" with its protocols and accrediting apparatus. In a segue from the lament psalms to pastoral care, the church has made two bargains. First, it has moved the indispensable truth-telling processes from the congregation into "private practice" so that the normative form has become one-on-one counseling. There are, to be sure, some remaining practices of group interaction as in recovery groups, but those tend to be at the margins of congregational life. The *privatism* of such pastoral care is most often done in a vacuum, as though the resources of the community did not matter to well-being.

Second, we have agreed to a *secular* form of truth-telling with a *human listener*, because the notion of *God as listener* is too embarrassing for us; we imagine that God is too timid or too fragile for such abrasive interaction. (I do not denigrate such a privatized secularized practice, because I have benefited greatly from such interaction.) But we may be aware that entrusted to us (and only to us) is a reliable script for a more public practice of voiced *I*'s who receive fresh valorization from this holy *Thou* who is made available through the practice of the congregation. Recovery of such public practice is, in my judgment, a powerful desideratum.

The other (less noble) strategy for scuttling the lament psalms is that the church has taken the full range of emotional needs and extremities and reduced them all to only one note, namely, guilt. Thus, liturgically the only aspect of the complex human self about which we regularly tell the truth is our guilt, in the regularity of confession. Moreover, we tend to do even that in rote, innocuous articulation. Such a singular accent reduces to silence all the other undeniable dimensions of the self that concern our life with each other and with God.

The contemporary Swedish interpreter Fredrik Lindström has carefully and compellingly shown that in the fifty or so lament psalms, there is not one admission of guilt: "It is highly doubtful if we can speak of a motif of sin in the individual Psalms. . . . The confession of sin is not an element in the classical individual complaint Psalms, and the motif of sin, in the few cases in which it occurs, hardly functions as indication of the reason for the affliction."[4]

In its lament-protest-complaint, Israel is not willing to accept responsibility for what has gone awry in its life. Often the fault is assigned to unnamed adversaries. Sometimes the fault is said to belong to God as the troublemaker through acts of infidelity toward Israel. It would be well, in my judgment, if the church moved beyond the silencing of these texts and created room in the liturgy for the full truth-telling of the diminished self.

Among other liabilities in an excessive focus on guilt is that it amounts to collusion with the political-economic oligarchy. That oligarchy of money and power is wont to "blame the victim" for his sorry state of disadvantage and vulnerability, when in fact the oligarchy itself is most often the perpetrator of such vexation for the vulnerable. Israel in its prayer will have none of that!

V

I suggest that the church would do well to recover the truth-telling processes of the lament psalms, because a greedy culture of despair will never make free and will never make well. The oligarchy, with its passion for control, predictably ends in despair, whereas the laments are acts of hope that God will make all things new.

In the "posthistory" of the laments, I refer to Luke 18:1–8, in which Jesus instructs his disciples to pray like a nagging widow who insists on justice before a cynical, indifferent judge. Her insistence on justice sounds very much like a lament psalm. When Jesus taught his disciples in this way, he might have said to these early Jewish followers, "Pray as you know to do in the lament psalms." Jesus does not promise that such prayer will be answered. Rather, he promises that with such prayer we will never "lose heart." Tepid practices of prayer, like so much prayer in the life of the church, end in denial about what dare not be uttered and become a sure way to "lose heart." What is required in order not to lose heart, in order to maintain hope, is engagement in self-announcement before one who reliably listens in a way that valorizes. The widow insists on being heard and finally is heard by the judge: "I will grant her justice, so that she may not wear me out by continually coming" (Luke 18:5).[5]

When the church loses heart and hope, its witness is tepid, its mission is weak, its courage is limited, and its imagination is domesticated. At the end of the text, Jesus wonders if the coming Son of Man will find faith on earth in humans praying as truth-tellers. That same question is put to us. How we answer it indicates a great deal about our practice of pastoral care. There is no other resource than the lament psalms that is so rich and inexorable in its prospect for truth-telling that makes for hope-filled well-being.

Homiletical Focus: "When Nagging Is Hoping"*

Prayer, on the one hand, seems like such a safe, innocuous thing to do, that you can do it without caring much or risking much. On the other hand, prayer seems largely a pious irrelevance in a world

---

Editor's note: What follows is a sermon, which Brueggemann preached on October 18, 1992, that interprets Jesus' parable of the Persistent Woman as an encouragement to hope and pray in ways that resemble the lament psalms. The lectionary texts for the day were Habakkuk 1:1–3; 2:1–4; Psalm 119:137–144; 2 Timothy 3:14–4:5; Luke 18:1–8.

indifferent to spiritual realities. In the Gospel of Luke, with such a demanding story as the Good Samaritan, and with such a tale of compassion as the Prodigal Son, we are surprised that Jesus takes up the issue of prayer as though prayer matters as much as the neighbor love of the Samaritan and as coming home to the waiting father. But as the text will make clear, Jesus has a very odd challenge in mind when he speaks of prayer.

I

Prayer, so the text asserts, is no ordinary, straightforward matter. So Jesus teaches us of prayer by telling a curious story. There was a nameless judge in a nameless city, a judge who had lots of power to rule and give out rewards and punishments. The judge was not in fact a credible or trustworthy figure. He did not fear God, and he did not respect human persons. He sounds like an indifferent public charlatan who got his office by calculation, and who had no passion for the duties of his office. He was just putting in his time and getting by. The problem of course was that he was the real authority. You could not get around him. You had to deal with him, even if his courtroom was an inhospitable place and you hated to go there.

In that same city, headed for his courtroom, was a widow, as nameless as the judge. She had a case against a neighbor. We are not told the nature of the case, but the story suggests that she was in the right. Now you must understand that in that ancient, patriarchal world, a widow is a nonperson. She has lost her husband, which means she has no rights and no power. She has lost her legal standing—no rights, no power, no clout, no way to make herself heard. You can tell that the story is a setup for a terrible transaction between an *indifferent judge* and a *worthless widow*. One would hardly imagine that she could ever get a fair hearing, let alone a just verdict. The judge did not fear God, let alone pay attention to the widow woman. The storyteller, Jesus, portrays the two characters in the most extreme form possible.

II

There is the unequal meeting in the courtroom. She files her petition. Denied! She files again, he denies again. She should rightly have been discouraged. No doubt as she left the courtroom, the judge thought, "Well, that's the last we will see of her." But the text says she "kept coming" to court. She kept coming to him, more demanding, more insistent, more shrill. She kept saying, "Give me the justice to which I am entitled!"

Well, you can imagine the reaction in the courtroom when she showed up again. She really is a pest. She probably is not well dressed. She does not talk right. She cannot afford a lawyer, so she presents her own case . . . poorly. The judge is exasperated. I imagine the clerk grins and rolls her eyes, to watch "your honor" wince once again and routinely deny the petition, yet one more time.

She should have been discouraged, enough to quit coming. But she has nowhere else to go. And she is convinced that she is right. So she keeps coming back. She makes no new arguments, but just says over and over: "Give me justice." What a nag!

Finally, after her sixteenth or twenty-fifth court appearance, the judge is exhausted. He is weary of her, and can find no way to discourage her further. She takes no hints from his indifference. So, just to get rid of her, the judge gives her what she wants. He grants her petition and gives her justice against her neighbor. She wins the case, because she has been a determined, relentless nag. She nagged because she had hope, not so much in the judge, but in the rightness of her claim. The outcome is credible. Nagging does indeed sometimes win!

III

But remember, this is a story about prayer. So Jesus comments on and interprets the story. He says, Notice what happened to the unjust judge. He is forced to give justice, not out of any desire, passion, or commitment, but in order to get a little peace and quiet.

Then Jesus says, in a very daring maneuver, You know, prayer to God is just like that unjust judge. Remember, this is not theology; it is a playful rabbinic story. But look how the story works.

You, we are the widow woman. Going into this court of prayer, we are not dressed well enough, we cannot speak well enough. We are an embarrassment to the court, but we keep coming in our resolve.

God. God is not all soft and gracious and romantic and loving. Imagine for a moment, God as the chief judge, in a seedy old gown, not paying much attention, bored to death, exhausted by these nag-gers that keep coming with all their endless, outrageous requests.

Prayer, says Jesus, is like that. It is a persistent transaction between a desperate widow and a cynical judge. The cynical judge might refuse to listen, and the desperate widow might go home defeated. Notice, however, that the outcome of this meeting does not depend upon the good inclination of the judge, but upon the pesky, cheeky persistence of the widow. She has no other resource and no alterna-tive to this judge who has power of life and death. This is in fact the court of last appeal. And she wins, by not giving in.

I hope you find this story as stunning and surprising as I do. You see, we are too romantic about prayer, thinking it is a happy little time between friends. Or we are too cynical about prayer, because we do not believe anything happens anyway, so we go through the empty motions. But both romanticism and cynicism miss the point, that everything from God depends upon the resolve and staying power of the widow woman.

IV

Let me observe three matters about the story and the comment of Jesus.

1. The woman is *filled with hope*. She would never, never, never quit, never, never give up or give in. She had hope because she knew she was legitimate in her asking. She had hope because she believed things could and would and must change. She had hope that the judge would rule for her, whether he liked her or not, because if he heard at all, the case is compelling. Prayer depends upon that kind of hope, that there is a God who has the power to create newness.

2. The *subject matter of this prayer is justice*. The term "justice" permeates this text: In the story, she says, "Grant me *justice*" (v. 3). The exhausted judge finally says, "I will grant her *justice*" (v. 5). In the comment upon the story, Jesus says, "God [will] grant *justice*" (v. 7). "He will quickly grant *justice*" (v. 8).

Justice is the right subject for prayer, since the image is of court-room and judge. We do well, however, to linger over the term "jus-tice." It is so much misunderstood in our disclosure, because we think it means only giving people what they deserve by their actions; so, punish bad people, starve lazy people. That, however, is not what the word means in the Bible. The Bible means by justice that everyone, because they live in the community, because they are human creatures, is entitled to all that is needed for dignity, peace, freedom, health, joy, and security. Caring, nagging people do not come before God with frivolous, selfish requests. But the subject of all serious prayer is to urge God to give justice, which means

> dignity for children,
> safety for families,
> homes for the homeless,
> schools for all learners,
> health care for all,
> food for the needy,
> support for the abused,
> compassion for those wearied too long,
> access for the disabled.

The Bible imagines that God will finally not let the world linger in inequity and inaccessibility. The church gathers, sometimes to pray for itself and our needfulness. But sometimes, in our rather comfortable churches, we have no overriding, desperate needs, and we go to court on behalf of others, to lift their cause for justice. We do that often, even when we do not think the judge will listen. We do so because Jesus says, "[P]ray always" (v. 1), pray to the judge for justice. When God is tired of it, and exasperated by our insistence, God will answer.

3. So nagging prayers for justice are indeed acts of hope. The naggers are filled with hope that justice can be done, that God will listen, that the world will be changed, that the widow will be honored. Then Jesus ends this lesson on prayer with the haunting, unanswered question: "When the Son of Man comes [the final great accounting of God], will he find faith on earth?" (v. 8). *At the bottom of hope and justice and nagging is faith.* Faith that this is God's world and God will listen, faith that the world will be changed. You see, in our secularized world, we do fall out of faith. We end in despair, believing that might makes right, that the problems are insoluble, that the world is so skewed that nothing finally can be changed. These widespread attitudes are in fact ways in which we give up on the fidelity and reality of God.

Prayer is not an occasion just for pious little children on their way to bed. Prayer is not simply for neurotic people who are excessively and sadly too religious. It is rather the core gesture by which we stay in faith, by which we hope for the world, by which we keep justice as the issue before God and ourselves. To "pray always" means to hope always for justice, to nag always the judge, to trust always in the power of God.

There really is no middle ground. Either, like the widow, we believe and hope and nag for justice. Or, says Jesus, we "lose heart" (v. 1). When we lose heart, we quit nagging and quit caring. We quit hoping and we quit trusting. And we settle in docility, for a world that will not and cannot change, and the problems of homelessness and poverty and all the rest are then accepted as permanent, intransigent realities.

The good news is that we baptized people are believers, hopers, and naggers for justice. We will not let God off the hook. God can be nagged to a good verdict. At bottom we are not prepared, we baptized people, to be resigned about ourselves, or our neighbor, or about injustice in the world. It is promised that if we do not lose heart, if we care endlessly, relentlessly, and passionately, God finally must care too. Pray always!

Questions for Reflection

1. The lament psalms show us that we can be honest with God about our pain, doubts, frustrations, anger, and more, and they offer us scripts to do so. These psalms set the stage for truth-telling in our lives. Does this change how you approach God? What are some truths that you want to lament to God?

2. The radical truth-telling in the lament psalms shows us that God is indeed with us and that God hears our cries. This can bring gladness, well-being, and renewal when we experience exhaustion. Have you experienced this gladness that Brueggemann calls the reconstitution of the self? After lamenting, do you experience this?

3. Brueggemann claims that many communities of faith have abandoned lament to create a polite spirituality that is individualized and privatized. Does public lamentation feature prominently in your own

faith community or church? How has truth-telling been stifled in your life and in the life of your community?

4. In the homiletic exposition of the story of the widow and the judge, we see a woman who is not afraid to pester and nag for justice. Jesus teaches that our prayers to God should be like this rather than romanticized and fluffy. How can you be like the widow and commit to pray wholeheartedly and insistently for justice, truth, and hope?

PART FIVE

Conclusion

Chapter 10

Embracing the Transformation

A Comment on Missionary Preaching

> *Understanding waits upon conversion, and the primary*
> *task of the newcomer is a missionary task: to offer a per-*
> *suasive account of a new moral or physical world. He must*
> *appear to the natives like an eagle at daybreak; they have*
> *their own owls.*[1]
> Michael Walzer, *Interpretation and Social Critique*

"Missionary preaching" is the voice of a "newcomer," one who has something dangerously new to say. "Missionary preaching" intends to make available to the listener the mission—the powerful mission of God in the world. That mission is an *assertion* of new reality wrought by God (*Gabe*, or gift), and an *invitation* to receive and participate in the new reality (*Aufgabe*, or task). In the pulpit at Columbia Theological Seminary, there is a sign for the eye of the preacher only. It says, "We would see Jesus."[2] The sign is the urgent request of the congregation that the preacher focus on making visible the new evangelical reality at work in the world. Less christologically articulated, the sign might say, "Show us the promised land," "Show us the power of God," "Tell us about the new world," "Announce the news that we may hope again."

I

Missionary preaching is simply (to quote Walzer) the "persuasive account of a new world" that is now available because God's purpose, God's intent, God's rule is now in effect. Conversely, the

153

power and claim of all other purposes and all old intentions have been broken. We need no longer live in fear or deference to those old powers, or hope for the gifts of those old regimes. The old has passed away; behold, the new has come (2 Cor. 5:17).

The central metaphor for this proclamation is the coming of God's governance, which displaces, nullifies, and delegitimates every other governance. Martin Buber has seen that the covenant meeting at Sinai was a daring act whereby the rule of Pharaoh was broken by the "Kingship of Yahweh."[3] The same break in power is dramatically asserted in Isaiah 40–55, when the governance of Babylon and of the Babylonian gods is broken by the rule of YHWH (see Isa. 46–47). In the New Testament, the Markan version of Jesus' self-announcement is a parallel assertion: "[T]he kingdom of God has come near; repent" (Mark 1:15). The hopeful invitations of Moses, Isaiah in exile, and Jesus, the invitation of the whole Bible, is to change the foundational loyalty of our life and to engage in this new loyalty that heals, liberates, and reconciles.[4] The mission of God is to overcome all such deathly powers. Preaching is the invitation to join in that overcoming, in order to have life. The central affirmation of every missionary sermon is that the power of deathliness has no more authority or claim over us. We are free for the loyalty appropriate to our life in the world.

II

An amazing fact about the Bible is that the Bible knows that this single, central, hopeful proclamation must be articulated in a rich, daring variety of ways. It will not do, either in the Bible or in our preaching, simply to reiterate a single formulation of the news, even if we like the sound of that formulation. When we use only a single formulation (or a few variants), the news becomes tired, boring, and reductionist. The challenge of preaching is that this well-known tale of God must be told as if it has never been heard before. The new land must be shown as if it has never been seen before.[5] That fresh telling and that new showing require disciplined, diligent imagination on the part of the preacher.

It is useful, I suggest, to pay attention to some of the central *thematic constructs* of the Bible that shape the assertion (*Gabe*) and the invitation (*Aufgabe*) in different ways. I will mention five such thematic constructs, which suggest that the Old Testament text is relentlessly rich and imaginative in articulating the new world of God for which we hope and in which we may live:

1. *Chaos is transformed into creation.* In its largest scope, the Bible invites us to think about God's transformation of the whole cosmos.[6] Much distorted missionary preaching is excessively personalist and privatistic, about "me and Jesus." How different if we think of Genesis 1 or Isaiah 65:17–25 as examples of missionary preaching! These poems assert the news that God has fashioned the chaotic, disordered world into a livable, ordered home (see Isa. 45:18–19). We are invited to terminate our complicity in the chaos (either causing chaos or enjoying it), in order to live freely on the terms of the life-giving order of God.

Conversely and even more boldly, the Bible speaks sweepingly about the old creation now hopelessly distorted, so that God works a wholly new re-creation. In the new world offered in these texts, old distortions of greed and anxiety are displaced by sharing and trust. Our preaching is to invite participation in a new creation that is offered as a livable home.

2. *Despair is overcome by God's promises moving toward fulfillment.* In his magisterial study of the Hexateuch, von Rad has shown how the literature of Genesis–Joshua is organized as the promise of God (Gen. 12:1–3) moving to the fulfillment of God (Josh. 21:43–45).[7] The life of Israel is fixed securely between sure promises and trusted fulfillments. Between the promise at the beginning and the fulfillment at the end, there is a hopeful buoyancy that knows that this flow of life is being kept, guarded, and guaranteed by God (cf. Heb. 11). The whole of the Hexateuch is preaching for "missionary work," because these texts present all of life under promise. They invite us to abandon our practice of hopelessness and futility, as though there were no promises and no fulfillments, as though life flatly depended on us. The text asserts we are no longer fated in a world of cosmic indifference, because there is a powerful destiny spoken over us that can be trusted.

3. *This world of harsh injustice is being urged to God's justice.* The story of Israel's monarchy (Samuel and Kings, the preexilic prophets) is a story of fearful self-serving power that is brutal and selfish. We find ourselves not far removed from such power, which works deep injustice and which seems set to last forever. But the text, through the voice of the prophets, gives account of another purpose, a purpose of care, compassion, and fidelity, which relentlessly protests against the brutality and finally has its way.[8]

This alternative account of Israel's life (told, for example, through the tale of Naboth's vineyard, or Hezekiah's prayer, or Amos's judgment, or Jeremiah's tears) asserts that Israel's life is not a flat, closed history. Israel's life is a demanding choice between two ways, one of which leads to life and one of which leads to death (cf. Deut. 30:15–20). In the context of the kings of Israel and Judah, this entire literature of kings and prophets is an exposé of injustice and an assertion that the rule of God's caring justice finally is the wave of the future. This sad story of the monarchy and the determined poetry of the prophets are together a summons to leave off old ways of manipulation and control, in order to hope in and embrace the possibility of communal justice appropriate to God's new rule.

4. *In a world of exile, there is a powerful impetus to come home.* The literature of the exile is a statement acknowledging what it is like to be displaced, alienated, and abandoned.[9] This earlier literature draws very close to the alienation of modern life. "Exile" is a pertinent metaphor for much of our present experience. The literature, however, does not dwell on the reality of exile, nor on the route into exile. It focuses rather on going home, on being cared for and led home by a God who fights for us like a warrior (Isa. 40:10) and who carries us gently like a mother (Isa. 40:11; 49:14–16).

5. *The wisdom of God is overcoming the foolishness of the world.*[10] The wisdom tradition of Proverbs and Job seems an unlikely locus for missional preaching. Yet even these texts bear witness to a different world where God governs.[11] The book of Proverbs is about the world of foolishness that brings death, a foolishness based in greed, selfishness, indifference, and the yearning for a "quick fix." The new world of God, offered as an alternative by the wisdom teachers, is one wisely ordered that yields life and well-being to those who are obediently discerning. The poem of Job, in a quite

different idiom, reflects on the killing, isolated outcome of a life lived in stultifying conformity (Job's friends) or in arrogant defiance (Job). The book of Job invites us to a different world, in which the wonder of God is visible and acknowledged (Job 38:1–41:34), and in which the terrible options of conformity and defiance are overcome (42:1–6).

These five categories are enormously suggestive and comprehend in a general way much of the text of the Old Testament.

- *Chaos* becoming *creation* or new creation (Gen. 1–11)
- *Despair* yielding to *promise* toward fulfillment (Genesis–Joshua)
- *Injustice* overridden by God's *justice* (Samuel, Kings, Prophets)
- *Exiles* invited *home* (exilic literature)
- *Foolishness* overcome by *wisdom* (Proverbs, Job)

This is not an exhaustive list of the theological-literary thematic constructs available in Old Testament literature, which are ways to present the new rule of God.[12] It is, however, a sufficient sample from which to observe the various ways in which the Old Testament lends itself to missional preaching. These theological-literary constructs are not yet the concrete stuff of preaching. They are only general models in which the texts are located, and they provide for us general interpretive clues. Three observations occur to me about this inventory.

First, there is *rich variety* in these constructs. No one of these thematics is more basic than another, though we may each have our favorite. Each makes its own peculiar statement and must be taken on its own terms. None should be flattened or reduced to sound like any others.

Second, each in its own way concerns the *transformative enterprise* of God that is under way, in which we are invited to hope and participate.

- Chaos is *being transformed* into creation.
- Despair is *being transformed* into fulfilled promises.
- Injustice is *being transformed* into a community of justice.
- Exile is *being transformed* into homecoming.
- Foolishness that kills is *being transformed* into wisdom that gives life.

In each case, the world is no longer what it was. The world is not as we thought it was, or as it appeared to be. A new world is, in the moment of the text (and our speech about the text), being offered and made available.

Third, these several thematic constructs are not flat descriptions or reports. They are rather *powerful appeals for us to discern the world differently*, to discern the world afresh, to receive a quite fresh perspective on the world through these particular articulations. The texts are not neutral observations, but they are powerful arguments that because of God's gospel, the world we live in is not the one we have been led to embrace.

III

We have moved in our analysis from *dominant metaphor* to *thematic constructs*. Now we make a second move toward greater specificity. What is preached is not a slogan about the new kingdom. What is preached is not a set of formal constructs. What is to be preached is the *specificity of the text* in order to permit *a weaned imagination*.

A. *The specificity of the text.* I assume that every missional sermon is the explication of a specific text as a peculiar presentation of a changed governance. I will suggest three examples of how we might move from *dominant metaphor* to *thematic construct* to *specific text*.

1. Micah 4:1–4
   (a) The dominant metaphor: *God's new rule*
   (b) The thematic construct: *chaos becomes creation*
   (c) The *specific text:*

> [T]hey shall beat their swords into plowshares,
>   and their spears into pruning hooks;
> nation shall not lift up sword against nation,
>   neither shall they learn war any more;
> but they shall all sit under their own vines and under
>   their own fig trees,
>   and no one shall make them afraid.[13]

> Mic. 4:3–4

We live in a world of chaos. Nobody needs more evidence for that. It is a world of greedy insecurity in which we want more and more fig trees and vines. We never seem to have enough to be satisfied. The reason we are driven by such greedy insecurity is that we have chosen to live by sword and spear, by weapons of aggression, intimidation, and brutality. The combination of greedy insecurity and weapons of brutality, of course, yields a world of chaos. They leave us very much afraid. The world is nonetheless being transformed. Creation is being made new. It is being made new in the very moment of this text. While we listen to the poem, we notice that fewer vines and fig trees might satisfy us, if only we begin to refashion our swords and spears into gardening tools to care for the earth and let it produce. The very poem and the sermon we preach are a part of the scenario of transformation. By the end of the poem, by the conclusion of the sermon, our weapons are slightly reshaped. We have had a slight move toward disarmament, not only in the big cold war, but in all the cold wars we fight every day. We find our chaos is a bit tamed. We have a glimpse of what it is like with God's new rule. We have a new hope and yearning that we could live, at home and everywhere, with "no one [to] make [us] afraid." We have now heard the invitation grounded in God's action.

2. Exodus 15:20–21
    (a) The dominant metaphor: *God's new rule*
    (b) The thematic construct: *despair transformed by God's promise*
    (c) The *specific text*:

> Then the prophet Miriam, Aaron's sister, took a tambourine in her hand; and all the women went out after her with tambourines and with dancing. And Miriam sang to them:
> "Sing to the LORD, for he has triumphed gloriously; horse and rider he has thrown into the sea."
> Exod. 15:20–21

We live, like ancient Israel, in a world of slavery, unreasonable expectations, and hopeless quotas. We are pursued by peer pressure, debts to be paid, social expectation, the daily drive for food. We endlessly produce, and it is never enough. That world of pressured production is deeply without hope, a dead place without promise. At the edge of that dead place, however, if we listen carefully, we can hear a new, faint piece of music that, while we listen, grows louder and more compelling. The music has an odd beat, the sound of liberated tambourines. We rush to the edge of the empire from where the sound is coming. When we arrive at the edge (where we never dared go before), we find our sister Miriam and many other sisters, dancing and singing with abandonment. Their bodies look exhausted from the accumulation of too much work and too much hopelessness.

But the tambourines summon their feet, and they cannot keep still, tired as they are. We watch their dance. Now they are not tired, because they are not in despair. They have slipped over the border of the empire and stand outside it. We listen to the song, and in the singing we hear the name of this God, YHWH, who is strong and powerful, who has drowned the horses, killed the warriors, ridden the sea—all the way to freedom.

We listen cynically to the song, because we are modern. We do not believe in silly miracles, because Pharaoh is forever. There are, moreover, no promises that the corporation has not co-opted. At least there is none known to us. Even in our cynicism, however, there is something haunting about the tambourine. Even more haunting is the look of rest and joy in the tired faces of the women, the sense of hopeful well-being and starting again that we never expected. The tambourines do not lie.

Even if the song is primitive, it is transformative. We begin a cautious foot-tapping and soon we have tentatively joined the song of freedom. The God who made the old promises has acted. The production quotas will no longer control our life—we sing all the way to freedom, and we will not again knuckle under to the quota and the pressure. It is strange, but the very song of Miriam (and the sermon we hear about the dancing) is itself the very process of transformation and liberation. The song sets us a little free, and we will never fully regress again. We have been at the edge of the empire, and we have looked outside the empire to the dance. We notice what it is like when we shake off the weight of despair and hope.

3. Proverbs 15:17
   (a) The dominant metaphor: *God's new rule*
   (b) The thematic construct: *wisdom overpowering foolishness*
   (c) The *specific text*:

   Better is a dinner of vegetables where love is
   than a fatted ox and hatred with it.
                                        Prov. 15:17

What we eat shapes our life. We have to watch what we eat. There are so many ways to be stupid about food. There are too many kinds of junk food, some cheap and greasy, some highly caloric, some exotic and costly. The more affluent we become, the more we imagine that every meal should be a rich feast. The more affluent we become, the more intense the social whirl, inviting and being invited, fed to exhaustion. We have to keep up appearances and return obligations. "We are going out and the sitter will fix pot pies for the children." The whirl leaves us exhausted. It is almost no fun anymore. But we cannot offend this fast style. "If we don't keep it up, we will be dropped, and anyway, the kids like the sitter better than us."

One way is fatted ox, seafood, prime beef, with exhaustion and alienation. Another way is to simplify, disengage, get healthy and slow down—eat greens, herbs, spinach. The alternative is not to "graze" but to eat, surrounded by a family with stories to tell and jokes to enjoy, laughs to share, hurts to pool, fears to embrace—"where love is." When a semblance of order returns to our consuming, the meal feels like the kingdom of God. The new rule has overwhelmed our hastened, desperate affluence concerning junk food and junk life. So we sing, "Forgive our foolish ways, Reclothe us in our rightful minds" with sane eating and caring.

The text is such a simple proverb. The patient, gentle discernment of what is "better," nevertheless, lets us leave off the killing foolishness. The proverb is unpacked at the dining room table in the presence of the whole family. The proverb transforms our foolish, deathly life into a feast of the kingdom—greens!

These three texts are so very different—Micah hoping, Miriam dancing, and Solomon advising. Each text bears a witness: Micah *from chaos to creation*, Miriam *from despair to promise*, Solomon *from foolishness to wisdom.* All three texts bear witness to the new rule of God, the new rule present in the text itself, a new world given in the act of our listening. In each rendering of the text, the preacher must attend to

(a) the central claim of a new governance;
(b) the thematic construct that shapes the transformation;
(c) the detail of image and the nuance of the text.

B. *A weaned imagination.* The purpose of a textual, missional sermon is to help listeners participate in the transformation God is now working, working in the process of the text and its proclamation. That is, the purpose of such a sermon is to let us be transformed. The sermon is not to talk about a transformation that happens somewhere else with someone else at another time. It is a transformation that happens now with us, here, in this moment of speaking and hearing (cf. Deut. 5:3). We need to ask: How do people like us change? How does transformation happen? While we do not know fully, this much seems clear. Serious preaching that evokes change aims not at doctrinal clarification or moral rectitude (either conservative or liberal), but at a weaned, newly authorized, and hope-filled imagination.

By "imagination" I mean the pictures, images, and metaphors we have in our heads that shape our world and determine our actions and values.[14] These images are elemental and preconceptual, having been acquired in prerational kinds of ways. They are not changed by rational argument. They are changed by being displaced by a more compelling set of images and narratives that have authority in our most elemental experiences.

When we belong to the old world—of chaos, despair, injustice, exile, and foolishness—we act out that world. If the world is perceived and experienced as chaos, we will act chaotically. We have been a long time learning to trust in and rely upon those *un*evangelical images of the world. Missionary preaching seeks to offer a more compelling set of images rooted in our deepest tradition and making contact with our memory and hope. Such preaching seeks eventually to wean our imagination away from the deathliness of a world where God does not govern.

Thus, for example, Micah's contemporaries lived in an imagined world of swords, spears, and greedy scarcity. Micah *imagined* with them a different world, a world of disarmament and contentment and security. He invited his listeners to live toward that alternative world. Miriam's contemporaries *imagined* a hopeless world of Pharaoh's brick quotas. Miriam and her sisters danced an alternative of promise and possibility, outside the scope of the empire. Solomon's greedy people *imagined* a world of junk food and junk living. The wisdom teacher *imagined* a "better" world, in each of these three cases; the new world offered is only an act of imagination, not more.

- The world of swords and spears still exists after Micah's poem, but we imagine pruning hooks and plowshares.
- The world of Pharaoh and bricks still exists after Miriam's dance, but we imagine tambourines, dancing, and freedom.
- The world of junk food still is seductive after Solomon's proverb, but we imagine a family happily gathered around spinach.

Little by little, our imagination can be weaned away from false "world proposals" that are the ideology and propaganda of the "rulers of this age." When our imagination is weaned away from falseness and death, the new rule of God has a chance. We imagine plowshares, tambourines, and spinach. On that basis, we hope differently, care differently, dance differently, eat differently—in a very different world, a world given us by the text.

IV

The text of course seems remote from our daily experience. It is the important, demanding task of the preacher to let the text touch in authoritative ways the concreteness of our imagination. The main claims of missional preaching, as I have suggested them, are:

(a) We live in a situation (world) that needs transformation.
(b) The news is that the decisive transformation has happened. (All these texts witness to that conviction.)
(c) We can participate in the unfinished business of the transformation by following the transformation wrought through the text;

by yielding our deathly images to be available for new
images given us in the gospel and its poetry;
by acting on the basis of the new claims of creation/
promise/justice/homecoming/wisdom.

The interpretive problem is this: How do I discern and experience this new reality given in the text? Missional preaching not
only makes an assertion. It issues an invitation. The invitation is to
relinquish the old world of death, to *embrace* the new world of life.
The drama of relinquishing and embracing is the crucial, ongoing,
unfinished drama of our life. For each of us, the invitation entails different actions and different transformation. But there is also a com-
monality about our situation. I suggest that in the United States, in
the next years of our preaching, the *relinquishment* to which we are
summoned is to break free of the *ideology of consumerism*, which
dominates our culture, and the allied *deception of militarism*, which
keeps us in bondage. Such a relinquishment is a tall order indeed,
perhaps one about which we have no agreement. What we probe for
is the concrete experience in our life of the power of chaos/despair/
injustice/exile/foolishness. I submit that the worldview of consumer
militarism (or conversely, militaristic consumerism) touches every
aspect of our life, engendering despair, fear, greed, and finally brutality among us.

Missional preaching is to make evident the deathliness of our
present idolatry and to present the good news of a counterreality.
This deathly power that besets us

- touches *public policy*, in terms of defense, welfare, taxation, and
  even our view of capital punishment;
- touches *interpersonal relations*, so that persons in marriage and
  family relations and in other face-to-face relations are treated as
  usable commodities or as conforming automatons;
- touches *personal self-concepts*, fostering a sense of needing to
  be either a consumer or a producer, ready to be hedonistic or
  useful, in either case debased from personhood and therefore
  increasingly numbed;
- touches our *perception of the world* as a cosmic orphanage where
  we live continually under enormous threat;
- touches our *view of God*, who is variously an awesome judge who
  punishes wrongdoing or a doting friend who is utterly tolerant.

Such an ideological view—chaotic as Micah's world, enslaving as Miriam's world, brutalizing as Solomon's foolish eaters—will destroy us.

The news to be proclaimed in missional preaching is that an alternative world is possible and offered because a faithful God rules.

- *Public policy* can be compassionate and caring, when free of the deathliness of militarism.
- *Other persons* can be friends and neighbors, when not pressured by utility.
- *The self* can be celebrated as a beloved, summoned heir of God, when we are freed of consumptive, productive models of self.
- *The world* can be appreciated as a network of life-giving forces, when exploitation of creation is stopped.
- *God* can be recognized as a faithful, generous, demanding partner, when our distortions of works righteousness and cheap grace are relinquished.

Every and any person can join the mission and share in the transformation. Any and every person can make important moves toward the new governance. We are invited into the transformation by "the renewal of [our] minds" (Rom. 12:2). The new governance, however, requires that we not be "conformed." Preaching is an imaginative empowerment for transformation, when our minds, hearts, and imagination are reinstructed.

V

The massive, hope-filled possibility in such preaching is that the world will be reperceived and reengaged as God's creation, now being freshly renewed. It is this settled but unfinished transformation that must be preached. In such preaching we assert:

The *truth* of the transformation. Missional preaching must affirm in as many modes and ways as possible that a new world of creation, promise, justice, homecoming, and wisdom has indeed begun.

The *hiddenness* of the transformation. It belongs to God's way that the new world comes like "a thief in the night," noticed only by those who watch for its coming. The loud, shrill power of the old world still fascinates us. We must be attentive to the alternative if we are to notice.

The *demand* of the transformation. The deep gift of God is free, but it is costly. No one enters this new world easily, casually, or accidentally. Entry requires an intentional embrace and a knowing relinquishment.

The *polemic* of the transformation. This preaching and the choices it requires are not "tolerant" or "evenhanded." The gospel is no friend of Pharaoh or death. The enemy is concretely named, and we must be prepared to name the deathliness that is operative in public policy, in our personal, intimate lives, and everywhere that we seek a newness.

The *joy and freedom* of the transformation. The assertion and invitation of missional preaching is an offer that we can now, as never before, become who we are meant to be, at peace, in joy, safe, cared for, hopeful, and empowered. This joy contrasts deeply and decisively with the failure of the living death all around us.

This chapter began with a wondrous quote from Walzer. There really is "a new world." That new world requires a "persuasive account." That new world requires that the preacher be "like an eagle at daybreak"—fresh, awesome, daring, sure, hopeful, and powerful. Too much of our preaching is like an owl at dusk—settled, wise, and dull; or like a pigeon at midnight—tired, unimpressive, fearful, sapped of energy. The transformation mediated in this text is for the congregation. It is, however, also for the preacher, that the preacher should be transformed from owl or pigeon to eagle. The text and the gospel intend that the preacher is one who may mount up on wings like an eagle, in order that the rest of us should

> run and not be weary,
> . . . walk and not faint.
> Isa. 40:31

When the eagle comes with a new world,
we shall dream with Micah,
we shall dance with Miriam,
we shall eat herbs with love.

The new world, birthed in the sermon that permits new hoping, new dreaming, new dancing, new eating, evokes new, joyous living.

We are then no longer conformed, but utterly transformed. Our minds are renewed, our lives are changed, and our world begins again.

Questions for Reflection

1. According to Walzer, missionary preaching is the persuasive account of a new world, in this case, the new world that is of God. This type of preaching imagines what that new world could be, while calling out the powers that hinder that world. If you were to preach in this way, what would you say? How might you imagine this new world and describe the powers that hinder it?

2. In this chapter, Brueggemann outlines five themes found throughout the biblical text that articulate the new world of God. Apply these themes to yourself, your community, our world, and our history. Where do you see chaos transformed into creation? Despair to promise? Injustice to justice? Exile to home? Foolishness to wisdom?

3. Each and every person can join in the missionary work of imagining a new world and creating that new world here on earth. The invitation is open. How do you invite people in your community to do this work? How do you empower and instruct people in their own gifts and talents to transform the world?

4. The work of missionary preaching is risky and daring, but powerful. This also means that this work is hard and draining. Throughout this journey of restoring hope and bringing about a new world, how will you sustain yourself? In what ways can you be intentional about caring for yourself and your communities through these difficult labors?

Acknowledgments

Chapters 1 and 2 include material from Walter Brueggemann, *Hope within History* (Atlanta: John Knox, 1987). Used by permission.

Chapter 1 includes material from Walter Brueggemann, *Reverberations of Faith: A Theological Handbook of Old Testament Themes* (Louisville, KY: Westminster John Knox, 2002). Used by permission.

Chapters 3, 5, 6, 7, and 8 include material from Walter Brueggemann and Tod Linafelt, *An Introduction to the Old Testament: The Canon and Christian Imagination*, 3rd ed. (Louisville, KY: Westminster John Knox, 2020). Used by permission.

Chapter 4 includes material from Walter Brueggemann, *Genesis*, Interpretation (Atlanta: John Knox, 1982), and Walter Brueggemann, *The Collected Sermons of Walter Brueggemann*, vol. 2 (Louisville, KY: Westminster John Knox, 2015). Used by permission.

Chapter 6 includes material from Walter Brueggemann, *From Judgment to Hope: A Study on the Prophets* (Louisville, KY: Westminster John Knox, 2019). Used by permission.

Chapters 7, 8, and 9 include material from Walter Brueggemann, *Truth and Hope: Essays for a Perilous Age*, ed. Louis Stulman (Louisville, KY: Westminster John Knox, 2020). Used by permission.

Chapter 9 includes material from Walter Brueggemann, *The Collected Sermons of Walter Brueggemann* (Louisville, KY: Westminster John Knox, 2011).

Chapter 10 includes revised material from Walter Brueggemann, "Embracing the Transformation: A Comment on Missionary Preaching," *Journal for Preachers* 11, no. 2 (1988): 8–18. Used by permission.

Notes

CHAPTER 1: THE BIBLE AS LITERATURE OF HOPE

1. Gerhard von Rad, *Old Testament Theology*, vol. 1, *The Theology of Israel's Historical Traditions*, trans. D. M. G. Stalker (New York: Harper & Row, 1962), 165–75. That the patriarchal narratives focus on hope is, of course, the main interpretive point of his Genesis commentary as well. Claus Westermann, *The Promises to the Fathers* (Philadelphia: Fortress, 1980).

2. David J. A. Clines, *The Theme of the Pentateuch*, Journal for the Study of the Old Testament Supplement Series 10 (Sheffield: University of Sheffield Press, 1978), 31–43, has helpfully summarized and categorized the data.

3. Albrecht Alt, "The God of the Fathers," in *Essays on Old Testament History and Religion* (Oxford: Blackwell, 1966), 1–66.

4. Paul Ricoeur, "Guilt, Ethics and Religion," in *The Conflict of Interpretations* (Evanston, IL: Northwestern University Press, 1974), 436–39. For the classic statement of Jürgen Moltmann, see *Theology of Hope* (New York: Harper & Row, 1967), chap. 2, on the distinction of promise and epiphany.

5. See the analysis of Hans Walter Wolff, "The Kerygma of the Yahwist," in *The Vitality of Old Testament Traditions*, ed. Walter Brueggemann and Hans Walter Wolff, 2nd ed. (Atlanta: John Knox, 1982), 46–55.

6. On the theological function of this narrative, see Walter Brueggemann, "'Impossibility' and Epistemology in the Faith Tradition of Abraham and Sarah (Gen. 18:1–15)," *Zeitschrift für die alttestamentliche Wissenschaft* 94 (1982): 615–34.

7. Gerhard von Rad, *Old Testament Theology*, vol. 2, *The Theology of Israel's Prophetic Traditions*, trans. D. M. G. Stalker (New York: Harper & Row, 1965), has considered these matters in detail; see esp. 263–77 on the new dimensions of prophetic hope in the sixth century.

8. See my discussion of the text, "'Vine and Fig Tree': A Case Study in Imagination and Criticism," *Catholic Biblical Quarterly* 43 (1981): 188–204.

9. See the argument of Hans Walter Wolff, "Micah the Moreshite—The Prophet and His Background," in *Israelite Wisdom*, ed. John G. Gammie (Missoula, MT: Scholars, 1979), 77–84. By his close attention to the text Wolff has

offered important support to the more general sociological perspective of American scholars.

10. On this passage see the analysis of Norman K. Gottwald, *All the Kingdoms of the Earth* (New York: Harper & Row, 1964), 222–28. More generally on the prophetic promises, see Thomas M. Raitt, *A Theology of Exile* (Philadelphia: Fortress, 1977).

11. That is the normal argument of scholars. See esp. Paul D. Hanson, *The Dawn of Apocalyptic* (Philadelphia: Fortress, 1975). A minority opinion is held by von Rad, *Old Testament Theology*, 2:301–8. See the review of various positions in the collection edited by Paul D. Hanson, *Visionaries and Their Apocalypses* (Philadelphia: Fortress, 1983).

12. See Michael Stone, *Scriptures, Sects and Visions* (Philadelphia: Fortress, 1980).

13. Martin Buber, *Kingship of God* (New York: Harper & Row, 1967), has seen this at the beginning of the current scholarly discussion. That is, the "kingdom" emerging out of Sinai was not simply a religious movement, but a political alternative in the world in which the category of obedience was decisive. Buber's work anticipated the later developments of Mendenhall and Gottwald. Buber's understanding at a very early time gave him a peculiarly critical posture over against political Zionism.

14. Sallie McFague, *Metaphorical Theology* (Philadelphia: Fortress, 1982), has shown how the metaphor of "kingdom of God" became crucial for the faith and literature of the faith community. The metaphor is at work in the parables of Jesus as in the Apocalypse, both of which are forms of imaginative, subversive literature.

15. On a radical reading of the prayer, see Michael Crosby, *Thy Will Be Done: Our Father as Subversive Activity* (Maryknoll, NY: Orbis, 1977). Sharon H. Ringe, *Jesus, Liberation, and the Biblical Jubilee* (Philadelphia: Fortress, 1985), shows how the Lord's Prayer is linked to the social hope of the jubilee year, which, of course, then has important political and economic implications.

16. On a most helpful proposal for penetrating to the common core of tradition and faith, see Paul van Buren, *Discerning the Way* (New York: Seabury, 1980). See also Markus Barth, *The People of God*, Journal for the Study of the New Testament Supplement Series 5 (Sheffield: JSOT, 1983), 25–26 and passim.

17. See the basic study of Richard R. Niebuhr, *Resurrection and Historical Reason* (New York: Charles Scribner's Sons, 1957), and the programmatic essay of W. B. Gallie, "The Historical Understanding," in *History and Theory*, ed. George H. Nadel (Middletown, CT: Wesleyan University Press, 1977), 149–202, on the theological method required by narrative.

18. Jürgen Moltmann has attempted to deal with this interface in his book *Hope and Planning* (New York: Harper & Row, 1971).

19. On relinquishment as an act of faith, see Marie Augusta Neal, *A Socio-Theology of Letting Go* (New York: Paulist, 1977).

20. See Moltmann, *Hope and Planning*, and M. Douglas Meeks, *Origins of the Theology of Hope* (Philadelphia: Fortress, 1974).

Notes 173

CHAPTER 2: LIVING TOWARD A VISION

1. See Walter Brueggemann, *Living toward a Vision* (Philadelphia: United Church, 1976), from which the title of this chapter is taken.

2. On "delegitimation" and social withdrawal of authority, see George E. Mendenhall, "The Hebrew Conquest of Palestine," in *The Biblical Archaeologist Reader 3*, ed. Edward F. Campbell Jr. and David Noel Freedman (Garden City, NY: Doubleday, 1970), 100–120. On the derivations made from that social act, see Norman K. Gottwald, *The Tribes of Yahweh* (Maryknoll, NY: Orbis, 1979), 408–9 and passim. John Swomley, *Liberation Ethics* (New York: Macmillan, 1972), has suggested how delegitimation and withdrawal function in the actual practice of radical ethics.

3. On the cruciality of imagination for liberation, see Frederick Herzog, "Liberation and Imagination," *Interpretation* 32 (1978): 227–41. Paul Ricoeur, in many of his writings, has understood the power of liberated imagination. See a succinct statement, "Philosophical Hermeneutics and Biblical Hermeneutics," in *Exegesis: Problems and Method and Exercises in Reading (Genesis 22 and Luke 15)*, ed. François Bovon and Gregoire Rouiller, Pittsburgh Theological Monograph Series 21 (Pittsburgh: Pickwick, 1978), 321–39.

4. See Paul D. Hanson, *The Dawn of Apocalyptic* (Philadelphia: Fortress, 1975), and, derivatively, Elizabeth Achtemeier, *The Community and Message of Isaiah 56–66* (Minneapolis: Augsburg, 1982).

5. On the political and symbolic futurity of the Daniel–Nebuchadnezzar literature, see W. Sibley Towner, "Were the English Puritans 'the Saints of the Most High'?," *Interpretation* 37 (1983): 46–63.

6. Herbert N. Schneidau, *Sacred Discontent: The Bible and Western Tradition* (Baton Rouge: Louisiana State University Press, 1977).

7. On the ideological containment of such intellectuals in the ancient world, see George E. Mendenhall, "The Shady Side of Wisdom: The Date and Purpose of Genesis 3," in *A Light unto My Path*, ed. Howard N. Bream, Ralph D. Heim, and Carey A. Moore (Philadelphia: Temple University Press, 1974), 319–34, and, less directly, Glendon E. Bryce, *A Legacy of Wisdom* (Lewisburg, PA: Bucknell University Press, 1979), esp. chaps. 7 and 8.

8. Gerhard Von Rad, *Old Testament Theology*, vol. 1, *The Theology of Israel's Historical Traditions*, trans. D. M. G. Stalker (New York: Harper & Row, 1962), 438–41, has noted six proverbs that speak against human control and with respect to the inscrutable mystery by which God governs. That, however, is against the main inclination of this literature. See also von Rad, *Wisdom in Israel*, trans. James D. Martin (Nashville: Abingdon, 1972), 98–110.

9. In addition to the writings of Mendenhall and Bryce cited in note 7, see Robert Gordis, *Poets, Prophets and Sages* (Bloomington: Indiana University Press, 1971), 160–97, and Brian W. Kovacs, "Is There a Class-Ethic in Proverbs?," in *Essays in Old Testament Ethics*, ed. James L. Crenshaw and John T. Willis (New York: KTAV, 1974), 171–89.

174   Notes

10. On the capacity of civility to effect social control and oppression, see Norbert Elias, *Power and Civility* (New York: Pantheon, 1982), and John M. Cuddihy, *The Ordeal of Civility* (New York: Basic, 1974).

11. See David Halberstam, *The Best and the Brightest* (New York: Random House, 1972). Those who served the government's effort in the Vietnam War were certainly not lacking in intelligence, but it became intelligence in the service of uncriticized power. The same thing happened with the agents of the Watergate cover-up. Reason that is contained uncriticized in the system is likely to be ideological, self-serving, and, finally, oppressive.

CHAPTER 3: THE OPEN-ENDED HOPE OF THE TORAH

1. Adele Berlin, "Numinous *Nomos*: On the Relationship between Narrative and Law," in *"A Wise and Discerning Mind": Essays in Honor of Burke O. Long*, ed. Saul M. Olyan and Robert C. Culley, Brown Judaic Studies 325 (Providence: Brown Judaic Studies, 2000), 25–31 (25, 30–31).

2. James M. Scott, *Exile: Old Testament, Jewish, and Christian Conceptions*, Journal for the Study of Judaism Supplement Series 56 (New York: Brill, 1997).

3. Jacob Neusner, *The Enchantments of Judaism: Rites of Transformation from Birth through Death* (New York: Basic Books, 1987).

4. Walter Brueggemann, *Deuteronomy* (Nashville: Abingdon, 2001), 81–93. See also Michael Fishbane, *Text and Texture: Close Readings of Select Biblical Texts* (New York: Schocken, 1979), 81–82.

5. Sara Little, *To Set One's Heart: Belief and Teaching in the Church* (Atlanta: John Knox, 1983).

6. James A. Sanders, "Adaptable for Life: The Nature and Function of Canon," in *Magnalia Dei, the Mighty Acts of God: Essays on the Bible and Archaeology in Memory of G. Ernest Wright*, ed. Frank Moore Cross, Werner E. Lemke, and Patrick D. Miller (Garden City, NY: Doubleday, 1976), 531–60.

7. Brevard S. Childs, *Introduction to the Old Testament as Scripture* (Philadelphia: Fortress, 1979).

8. Martin Noth, *A History of Pentateuchal Traditions*, trans. Bernard W. Anderson (Englewood Cliffs, NJ: Prentice-Hall, 1972); Gerhard von Rad, *Old Testament Theology*, vol. 1, *The Theology of Israel's Historical Traditions*, trans. D. M. G. Stalker (New York: Harper & Row, 1962).

9. James A. Sanders, *Torah and Canon* (Philadelphia: Fortress, 1972).

10. As was suggested by Rudolf Bultmann, "The Significance of the Old Testament for the Christian Faith," in *The Old Testament and Christian Faith: A Theological Discussion*, ed. and trans. Bernhard W. Anderson (New York: Harper & Row, 1963), 8–35.

11. Martin Noth, *The Deuteronomistic History*, Journal for the Study of the Old Testament Supplement Series 15 (Sheffield: JSOT, 1981).

12. Frank Crüsemann, *The Torah: Theology and Social History of Old Testament Law*, trans. Allan W. Mahnke (Minneapolis: Fortress, 1996).

13. Samuel E. Balentine, *The Torah's Vision of Worship*, Overtures to Biblical Theology (Minneapolis: Fortress, 1999), 240.

CHAPTER 4: GOD'S PROMISES AND PROVISION

1. Karl Barth, *Church Dogmatics* III/1:41; IV/1:57 (Edinburgh: T. & T. Clark, 1958–60).

2. Claus Westermann, "Types of Narratives in Genesis," in *The Promises to the Fathers* (1964; repr., Philadelphia: Fortress, 1980), 71–73.

3. Hans Walter Wolff, "The Kerygma of the Yahwist," trans. Wilbur A. Benware, *Interpretation* 20 (1966): 131–58. Reprinted in *The Vitality of Old Testament Traditions*, by Walter Brueggemann and Hans Walter Wolff, 2nd ed. (Atlanta: John Knox, 1982), 41–66.

CHAPTER 5: THE PROPHETS

1. David Noel Freedman, *The Unity of the Hebrew Bible* (Ann Arbor: University of Michigan Press, 1991), 1–39.

2. Gerhard von Rad, *The Problem of the Hexateuch and Other Essays*, trans. E. W. Trueman Dicken (New York: McGraw-Hill, 1966), 1–78.

3. David L. Petersen, *The Prophetic Literature: An Introduction* (Louisville, KY: Westminster John Knox, 2002), 1–45 and passim.

4. James Nogalski, *Redactional Processes in the Book of the Twelve*, Beihefte zur Zeitschrift für die alttestamentliche Wissenschaft 218 (Berlin: de Gruyter, 1993); Paul R. House, *The Unity of the Twelve*, Bible and Literature Series 27 (Sheffield: Almond, 1990); James Nogalski and Marvin A. Sweeney, eds., *Reading and Hearing the Book of the Twelve*, Society of Biblical Literature Symposium Series 15 (Atlanta: SBL, 2000).

5. Brevard S. Childs, *Introduction to the Old Testament as Scripture* (Philadephia: Fortress, 1979), 325–38.

6. Walther Zimmerli, *The Law and the Prophets: A Study of the Meaning of the Old Testament* (Oxford: Blackwell, 1965).

7. Eric Voegelin, *Order and History*, vol. 1, *Israel and Revelation* (Baton Rouge: Louisiana State University Press, 1956).

8. See Rolf Rendtorff, "How to Read the Book of the Twelve as a Theological Unity," in *Reading and Hearing the Book of the Twelve*, ed. James Nogalski and Marvin A. Sweeney (Atlanta: SBL, 2000), 75–87.

9. Ronald E. Clements, "Patterns in the Prophetic Canon," in *Canon and Authority: Essays in Old Testament Religion and Theology*, ed. George W. Coats and Burke O. Long (Philadelphia: Fortress, 1977), 42–55 (48, 49).

10. Clements, "Patterns in the Prophetic Canon," 53.

CHAPTER 7: HOPE TRANSFORMED IN THE WRITINGS

1. Donn F. Morgan, *Between Text and Community: The "Writings" in Canonical Interpretation* (Minneapolis: Fortress, 1990).

2. Michael E. Stone, *Scriptures, Sects, and Visions: A Profile of Judaism from Ezra to the Jewish Revolts* (Philadelphia: Fortress, 1980).

3. See Morgan, *Between Text and Community*, 71, 40.

4. See Morgan, *Between Text and Community*, 53.

5. Jacob Neusner, *The Enchantments of Judaism: Rites of Transformation from Birth through Death* (New York: Basic Books, 1987).

6. Jack Miles, *God: A Biography* (New York: Simon & Schuster, 1995); see also Richard Elliott Friedman, *The Disappearance of God: A Divine Mystery* (Boston: Little, Brown, 1995).

7. John J. Collins, *The Apocalyptic Vision of the Book of Daniel* (Chico, CA: Scholars Press, 1976), 84–85. I am indebted to Daniel Smith-Christopher for this reference.

8. Daniel L. Smith, *The Religion of the Landless: The Social Context of the Babylonian Exile* (Bloomington, IN: Meyer-Stone, 1989), 164.

9. Smith, *Religion of the Landless*, 8, quoting Nelson H. H. Graburn, ed., *Ethnic and Tourist Arts: Cultural Expression from the Fourth World* (Berkeley and Los Angeles: University of California Press, 1976), 1.

CHAPTER 8: HOPE IN GOD'S FUTURE, GROUNDED IN HOLINESS

1. Daniel Smith-Christopher, *A Biblical Theology of Exile*, Overtures to Biblical Theology (Minneapolis: Fortress, 2002), 145–88.

2. Susan Jacoby, *The Age of American Unreason* (New York: Penguin, 2008), chapter 9 and passim, considers the way in which "junk thought" has eroded critical capacity in US culture. Her notion of junk thought, it seems to me, is very like the yeast of the Pharisees and the yeast of Herod, about which Jesus warns (Mark 8:15).

3. This statement calls to mind the earlier poetic lines from Isa. 55:1–2 that offer free food and then ask, in a tone of reprimand, "Why do you labor for that which does not satisfy?" The contrast in those verses between real food and junk food is parallel to being thirsty and never thirsting again.

4. John J. Collins, *The Apocalyptic Imagination: An Introduction to the Jewish Matrix of Christianity* (New York: Crossroad, 1987), 68–92.

5. W. Sibley Towner, *Daniel,* Interpretation (Atlanta: John Knox, 1984), 104.

6. Towner, *Daniel*, 105–6.

7. George Nickelsburg, "Son of Man," in *Anchor Bible Dictionary,* ed. David Noel Freedman (New York: Doubleday, 1992), 4:142–50.

8. Patrick D. Miller, *Genesis 1–11: Studies in Structure and Theme* (Sheffield: JSOT, 1978), 9–26.

9. Martin Noth, *The Laws in the Pentateuch, and Other Studies*, trans. D. R. Ap-Thomas (Philadelphia: Fortress, 1967), 228.

10. Samuel E. Balentine, *Prayer in the Hebrew Bible: The Drama of Divine-Human Dialogue* (Minneapolis: Fortress, 1993), 108–9.

CHAPTER 9: THE NAGGING HOPE OF THE LAMENT PSALMS

1. See Walter Brueggemann, *From Whom No Secrets Are Hid: Introducing the Psalms,* ed. Brent A. Strawn (Louisville, KY: Westminster John Knox, 2014).

2. On the cruciality of an experience of omnipotence for personal health, see D. W. Winnicott, *The Maturational Processes and the Facilitating Environment: Studies in the Theory of Emotional Development* (Madison, CT: International Universities Press, 1965), 180 and passim.

3. See Walter Brueggemann, "The Costly Loss of Lament," in *The Psalms and the Life of Faith* (Minneapolis: Fortress, 1995), 98–111.

4. Fredrik Lindström, *Suffering and Sin: Interpretations of Illness in the Individual Complaint Psalms* (Stockholm: Almqvist & Wiksell International, 1994), 350.

5. John R. Donahue, *The Gospel in Parables* (Philadelphia: Fortress, 1988), 183, translates the response of the judge this way: "Because this widow is 'working me over' I will recognize her rights, so she doesn't give me a black eye by her unwillingness to give up.'"

CHAPTER 10: EMBRACING THE TRANSFORMATION

1. Michael Walzer, *Interpretation and Social Criticism* (Cambridge: Harvard University Press, 1987), 44. Walzer is speaking generically about the missionary task of any missionary and not specifically about the Christian mission.

2. In a church where I preached recently, the sign for the eyes of the preacher only said, "Don't Move the Microphone." I could not detect a christological intention in that expression.

3. Martin Buber, *The Kingship of God* (London: Allen & Unwin, 1967).

4. After having written this paragraph, I am aware that these three articulations echo the dramatic shaping of the material by Bernhard W. Anderson, *The Unfolding Drama of the Bible*, 4th ed. (Minneapolis: Fortress, 2006).

5. On the prospects for this demanding responsibility, see Fred B. Craddock, *Overhearing the Gospel* (Nashville: Abingdon, 1978).

6. See Bernhard W. Anderson, *Creation versus Chaos: Reinterpretation of Mythical Symbolism in the Bible* (1967; repr., Eugene, OR: Wipf & Stock, 2005).

7. Gerhard von Rad, "The Form-critical Problem of the Hexateuch," in *The Problem of the Hexateuch and Other Essays*, trans. E. W. Trueman Dicken (New York: McGraw-Hill, 1966), 1–78.

8. See Walter Brueggemann, *The Prophetic Imagination: 40th Anniversary Edition* (Minneapolis: Fortress, 2018).

9. See Ralph W. Klein, *Israel in Exile* (Philadelphia: Fortress, 1980).

10. This formulation is, of course, an inversion of 1 Cor. 1:18–25. The inversion is required because, in the end, it is God's foolishness that is wise.

11. See Gerhard von Rad, *Wisdom in Israel*, trans. James D. Martin (Nashville: Abingdon, 1972).

12. Among the other thematic constructs that might be discussed are (a) the move from lament to praise in the Psalms; (b) tales of inversion in the books of Genesis, Numbers, and Kings; and (c) apocalyptic anticipations in Zechariah and Daniel.

13. The entire poetic unit of verses 1–4 (5) must, of course, be treated. Because of space limitations, I have quoted only a portion of the unit.

14. See John Coulson, *Religion and Imagination: "In Aid of a Grammar of Assent"* (Oxford: Clarendon, 1981).

CPSIA information can be obtained
at www.ICGtesting.com
Printed in the USA
LVHW021247310323
743100LV00003B/6

9 780664 265908